A Metaphysics
of the
Christian Mystery

BRUNO BÉRARD

A Metaphysics
of the
Christian Mystery

An Introduction to the
Work of Jean Borella

Angelico Press

CONTENTS

FOREWORD

DID IT EVER HAPPEN THAT YOU STARTED READING
a book and suddenly felt that you had written the book yourself? This is what
happened to me in my encounter with Jean Borella's work. I felt at home;
I entered into his thought as if it were my own. Even what I could never
have imagined beforehand came to me as an experience of *déjà vu*. It was a
tremendous, incredible experience.

After purchasing one of Borella's books (now available in English translation
under the title *Christ the Original Mystery*), I decided to write a summary of it
and submitted it to the author. His response was so positive that I committed
myself to the project of summarizing all of the books he had written up to
that time, consisting of some three thousand five hundred pages, condensing
them to about three hundred and fifty pages, with the additional challenge
of bringing out the *integrality* of his thought.

After long — but happy — hours, weeks and years, the book was published,
with a postface by Borella confirming its accuracy and relevance. Unique in
existing literature, it has proven popular among Borella's French readers as a
guide through the doors of his opus and a highlighting of what is most essential.[1]

For this reason Angelico Press has opted to publish, alongside a number of
Borella titles, the present abridgment and translation of the original adapted
to the needs of a more general though predominantly Catholic audience.

---

1 *Jean Borella. La Révolution métaphysique après Galilée, Kant, Marx, Freud, Derrida*
(Paris: l'Harmattan, 2006).

INTRODUCTION

JEAN BORELLA IS NOT A CHRISTIAN PHILOSOPHER, a philosopher who happens to be Christian: he is, rather, a Christian who happens to be a philosopher.[1] And this fact is crucial: it affects the very essence of his philosophic thought. Indeed, to be a philosopher can be merely a profession, a hobby even, or an intellectual game; but to be a Christian demands at the very least an awareness of transcendence and of a Revelation. And this entails an *orientation* of one's being, an *essence* as opposed to an accident, as Aristotle would say. As such, it marks the difference between *principles* and ideologies: whereas principles *govern*, ideologies are merely rationalizations, mental constructs that can justify virtually anything, down to murders and infanticides. As Borella points out, ideologies can 'theoretically establish' and 'emotionally justify' social, political, aesthetic or ethical norms and 'provide them with the ideo-psychic nourishment they need to endure'. And as a matter of fact, ideologies constitute 'the true mythologies of the modern world'.[2] Any philosophy, moreover, disconnected from its roots (from the enigmatic question 'Why and how do I think?') runs the risk of being reduced to an ideology.

Borella's thought is not confined to some formal structure; it continually expands its global compass. And yet in its essence it is centered on an idea that serves as a universal key: namely that of the *symbol*. "The symbol activates thought," says Paul Ricoeur; Borella broadens and deepens this insight: "the symbol not only 'gives food for thought' but even endows thought with its very self";[3] it reveals reality, and indeed it is "the notion of the symbol which lets us *think* the notion of reality."[4]

---

1 *Symbolism and Reality*, 430. English translation published in the same volume as *The Crisis of Religious Symbolism* (Kettering, OH: Angelico Press/Sophia Perennis, 2016).
2 *The Sense of the Supernatural* (Edinburgh : T & T Clark, 1998), 1.
3 *Symbolism and Reality*, 426.
4 Ibid., 421.

A Metaphysics of the Christian Mystery

What does this mean? No one would deny that despite the stupendous proliferation of rational constructs, be they philosophical or scientific, there remains as a mystery the question 'Why is there something rather than nothing?', as Leibniz has put it,[5] and the hope to reach the ultimate truth, the 'beyond' of things that is metaphysical reality. And this is where the symbol comes into play: it is needed to break through the confines of our conceptual prison by opening a way to transcendent reality. To access reality one needs to depart from the world of words and thoughts. There are however only two ways to stop thinking: by action, namely, or by contemplation. The first corresponds to the way of science, which attains its end in 'prediction and control', and thus basically with technology, whereas the second is the way of metaphysics, the end of which is no less than the contemplation of reality. To reach its true objective philosophy must thus transcend its own constructs, relinquish its own logic and its very thought in order to take possession of that which is beyond logic, beyond all thought.

The reality of the symbol can only be demonstrated by a *reductio ad absurdum.* By virtue of its transcendence — the fact that it is not merely a thought or a concept — the reality of a symbol, that is to say its existence, can only be demonstrated indirectly by showing that its denial by way of a pure rationalism proves to be contradictory. And this is the task Borella set himself in *The Crisis of Religious Symbolism.* From Galileo's physical materialism — the concept of the Galilean universe — all the way to the Derridian structuralism by way of the Kantian *Kritik,* the sociologism of Marx and Feuerbach, and the psychologism of Freud, he has demonstrated the contradiction inherent in each of these philosophies, thereby showing the spurious nature of any thought (*logos*) when it is disconnected from its roots (*mythos*). The broad lines of this reasoning are as follows:

- To deny the transcendence of sacred forms (symbols) — to deny that these are in effect messages from beyond the conceptual world — is to reduce these forms to productions of the human unconscious mind.
- But if such is the general rule for the universal process which alienates minds from the real, how is it possible that some minds are spared from that alienation?

5 *Principle of Nature and of Grace based on Reason* (1714), § 7.

- The 'illusion of the sacred' is therefore neither structural nor universal, and one has failed to establish the so-called 'ineluctable alienation of religion' on structural or universal grounds.
- This in turn lays bare the pretentiousness and fallacy of philosophers who presume to have eluded an alienation declared universal.

How does the symbol operate, and why does it 'work'? A symbol connects the visible to the invisible by virtue of a 'dissimilar similarity' (René Roques). More precisely, similarity constitutes the static link of a connecting analogy, whereas dissimilarity betokens the anagogic power[6] of the symbol by which the ascent from image to Archetype is effected (Borella).

"God perceives the world in Himself," declares St. Thomas Aquinas;[7] and by this all-inclusive vision He knows all things. And, as Borella notes, in thus knowing them He "cognitively draws them out of their own mode of existence, for it is precisely by this mode — by the limitation that constitutes a particular mode of being — that they are distinguished and separated from the principle. To exist (from *ex sistere*) is to 'stand out' from perfect reality and so lapse towards nothingness."[8] Now, what prevents this fall from being completed and consequently renders existence possible is the opposing attraction effected by the divine Knowing, through which all things are united to the Principle by way of their archetypes. "Here we see knowledge converted into being in precisely the same way that being is converted into knowledge. . . . The symbol, then, is the memorial of the all-encompassing Knowledge of God, and thus of the metaphysical nature of the cosmos, the omnipresence therein of the *Logos*."[9]

Intelligence is thus burdened with an imperative: it must *be converted to the symbol.* There *is* simply *no* rational alternative, no other way to escape from the 'monster' of self-contradiction than to be thus converted: to allow symbols to *lead*, to follow them in their interrogation of reality and, as Borella expresses it, "to enter with [them] into the metaphysical conversion of the real to which [they] welcome us, to be open to the transfiguration of the world's

6 The act of *anagogy* (from *ana* + *agein*) is quite literally a 'leading upwards'.
7 *Summa Theologiae* I, Quest. 14, Art. 5.
8 *Histoire et théorie du symbole* (Lausanne: L'Age d'Homme, 2004), 235.
9 Ibid., 235 ff.

A Metaphysics of the Christian Mystery

flesh of which [symbols are] the prophetic witness and the salvific allure."[10]
And most significantly, as he says elsewhere:

> [In this conversion] the conflict of faith and reason, of the uni-
> versality of the *logos* confronted with the contingency of religious
> cultures, is resolved: here meaning is united with being, the
> non-formal intellect is united with sacred forms, dead in them-
> selves but resurrected in their transfiguration. To the impossible
> speculative *suicide* of a reason illusorily demystified corresponds
> the *sacrifice* of an intellect that finds its fulfillment only in the
> crucifying mediation of the symbol, as exemplarily taught in the
> mystery of the paschal Night.[11]

Here 'science' gives way to *nescience*: because, to enter that 'superknowing',
the Pauline *epignosis,* "one must renounce all knowledge, even the knowledge
of Ideas."[12] And this means that "the metaphysical intelligence must engage
concretely in an act of faith in the revealed God: without Revelation, no
divine Object." And most importantly:

> . . . without the divine Object shining in the night of our exis-
> tence, no possible salvation, since in that case any pilgrimage to
> such an absent light is *precluded.* The intelligence must enact a
> kind of *sacrificium intellectus*; it must entomb itself in faith as in
> the death of Christ-*Logos*, but only so to rise again with Him.[13]

What follows, as well as what has been thus far explained, is simply the
thought of Jean Borella, his philosophy as given in his extensive writings. In this
book, this abridgment, we have however made a selection aimed at presenting
those aspects of Borella's opus that relate most directly to *the metaphysics of
the Christian mysteries*, while serving at the same time as a brief introduction
to his philosophy as a whole.

---

10   *The Crisis of Religious Symbolism*, 429.
11   Ibid., 9.
12   *Penser l'analogie* (Geneva: Ad Solem, 2000), 189.
13   Ibid., 189, n. 25.

PART I

Gnosis
&
Theology

ONE

Intelligence & Reason,
the Psychic & the Spiritual

INTELLIGENCE AND REASON

When thinking about subjects related to God, it is still necessary, until a doctrine of symbolic realism finds a welcome in modern minds, to discuss the compatibility of theology (as the science—logos—of God—Theos) with intelligence and reason.

Borella's Lumières de la théologie mystique *[Insights into Mystical Theology] offers us the opportunity to deal with this compatibility (Article 1: Theology and intelligence) and, further, to draft a history of the dictates of reason (Article 2: Theology and reason).*

Theology and Intelligence

'Science' (in the sense of a conceptually rigorous discourse) and theology are not mutually exclusive. To deny this would reduce the understanding of all sciences solely to an understanding of empirical realities. Now no science can be restricted in this way, in view of those theoretical constructs and speculations necessary for its development. And so one might even say that the noblest Object of our intelligence is "the ultimate speculative confrontation with the Beyond of all things." This is where our intellect "decisively and paradoxically experiences its own limits and suddenly discovers in itself a true capacity for contemplative adoration."[1]

While up to this point it would seem quite reasonable to allow science (even the science of God) the right to rigor as well as to ultimate speculation, however, to say that intelligence is "a true capacity for contemplative

---

1 *Lumières de la théologie mystique* (Lausanne: L'Age d'Homme, 2002), 10–11.

adoration" might seem quite surprising. And yet, even though this cannot be proven, anyone can experience it. Such theology is then much more than a simple discourse (*logos*) about God. It involves an actual spiritual way, which, in this sense, bears the name *mystical theology*, the ultimate theology towards which all theology leads.[2]

For the moment, then, we can say that theology is entitled to intelligence — but to reason?

Theology and Reason

Reason must first be distinguished from intelligence. Although these two faculties are only one—according to St. Thomas Aquinas—reason is the act of discursive thinking, while *intellect* enables us to intuitively and inwardly fathom the truth. Reason is "the power of judging and distinguishing truth from error,"[3] "the linking together of truths,"[4] while to intelligence corresponds the faculty of understanding: intellection. In other words, it is one thing to reason, another to understand the reasoning. This proximity of meanings is in any case enough, once the theologian is *allowed* to be intelligent, to afford him the right to reason as well. Theology can be then both an intelligent and reasonable work as to its *form* or methods; at the most, only its *matter* (its Object) could be disputed.

But is this true? Could such a dispute be legitimate? Is it enough that everyone still opposes *natural reason* to *supernatural revelation*, for this pair to give structure to any theological problematic? In particular, should whatever does not explicitly come from God (Revelation) necessarily come from man (reason)? Can reason function solely on its own resources and according to its own requirements?

This opposition is in fact only a point of view, formalized since the Middle Ages and linked to the Aristotelianization of philosophy, when the thirteenth century discovered the existence of a pagan philosophy which, ignoring revelation, could still attain the knowledge of truths relating to God and the conduct of human life.[5] According to the Aristotelian conception, "the

---

2 This is discussed in chapter 3.
3 Descartes, *Discourse on the Method*, I.
4 Leibniz, *Theodicy*, discourse 1.
5 Borella, *Lumières de la théologie mystique*, 58 ff.

specific and proportionate activity of human reason is a scientific knowledge
of the perceptible world" and the formality of scientific discourse (syllogistic
logic) guarantees its rigor. However, "for the Platonic noetic, the object
is the basis for the truth of knowledge. . . . The intellect, in its *desire* for
perfect knowledge is thus a wellspring governed by the contemplation of
unconditioned Reality, the Good in itself." Only faith can bring before the
intellect, "in the darkness of the Cavern, those intelligible objects that it will
later know in its ascent to the light of the Divine Sun, up to that supreme
Object beyond every object."[6]

Reason, as expressed by the main principles of the understanding and
pure (Aristotelian) logic, actually is, as a cognitive instance, *formally* universal. But, as considered in itself, this pure reason is only an abstraction;
it is pure "in its timeless universality as long as it is applied to nothing
and is of no use."[7] *Materially*, that is, as soon as it is applied to specific
materials, reason must come to terms with them and comply with them.
This is why, according to place and time-period, according to the culture
that is matrix for perceptible and intellectual experiences, there are distinct
systems of rationality. This so highly celebrated *natural reason* is rather a
cultural reason. And this is why there is a history of reason, which, quite
approximately, seems to exhibit four phases or four systems of rationality,
at least in the West:[8]

1. "The Platonic system of an intellective reason hierarchically ordered
   to the divine,
2. the Aristotelian-Thomistic system of a logical reason subject to
   revelation, but still imbued with intellectuality,
3. the Kantian system of a scientifico-critical reason, horizontally
   aligned with religious beliefs,
4. the [Derridian] cybernetic or combinatorial system of a decon-
   structed and decentered reason, abandoned to the power of its
   economic, social or ethnologic determinations."[9]

6 Ibid., 84.
7 Ibid., 60.
8 Ibid., 60–1.
9 Ibid.

SYSTEMS	1	2	3	4
	PLATONIC	**ARISTOTELIAN-THOMIST**	**KANTIAN**	**DERRIDIAN**
	5TH–4TH C. B.C. (then 2ND–5TH C., then *Quattrocento*)	5TH C. B.C. and 13TH C. (then 15TH–19TH C.)	18TH C. (then 19TH–20TH)	20TH C. (then 21ST?)
REASON	Intellective and ordered to the divine	Subject to revelation	Aligned with religions	Deconstructed and decentered

Now what is interesting is to compare the relative autonomy or heteronomy of reason within these systems:

- Systems 2 and 3 both imply the relative autonomy of a so-called natural reason, because it is distinct from the supernatural or religious order, but go in opposite directions: autonomy of service and subordination as a means to the end that utilizes it in the case of system 2; autonomy of independence, or even revolt, dedicated to a freeing from superstitions subjugating reason in that of system 3.

- Similarly, systems 1 and 4 imply a relative heteronomy of reason, but, again, in opposite directions: the combinatorial reason (the Derridian decentering of the *logos*) is subject to the hazards of its socio-cultural or psychoanalytic conditioning, thus to what is infrarational and alienating, while intellective (Platonic) reason is subject to the grace of what René Roques calls its 'transcendent conditioning',[10] thus to what is superior to it and completes it.

- We can see then how systems 1 and 2 are related: transcendent conditioning plays a revelatory role with respect to reason in system 2, while mystical intellection plays this role in system 1. They are probably combined in ancient, that is to say sacred cultures — cultures that claim a divine origin lost in the mists of time, that harken back to a primitive revelation.[11]

---

10 René Roques, *L'Univers dionysien* (Paris: Aubier, 1954), 217; Borella, *Lumières de la théologie mystique*, 61.

11 *Lumières de la théologie mystique*, 61.

SYSTEMS	1 PLATONIC	2 ARISTOTELIAN-THOMIST	3 KANTIAN	4 DERRIDIAN
REASON	Intellective and ordered to the divine	Subject to revelation	Aligned with religions	Deconstructed and decentered
Relative autonomy of reason		Autonomy of service but *subject to* *revelation*	Autonomy of independence, even revolt	
Relative heteronomy of reason	Subject to grace			Subject to the hazards of its conditioning
Relative equivalence of subordination	Transcendent Conditioning			
	Mystical intellection	Revelation		
	Probably combined in sacred cultures			

We conclude this outline with a crucial point: "there is no such thing as . . . an exclusively secular and entirely natural reason." This includes Kantian reason, whose apparent autonomy is based on the exclusion of intellectual intuition, after Kant reduced it to an example of perceptible intuition.[12] As far as Derridian reason is concerned, it seems to follow the work of structural anthropology, claiming, contrary to a unitary concept of reason, that there is a "heterogeity, in space and time, of thinking forms reduced to the contingency of simple arrangements or combinations of elements." But "if this were true, then no thinking at all could *rationally* voice such assertions. Reason is one or it is not."[13]

Thus, not only does theology reason intelligently, but, what is more, reason is a faculty naturally adapted to theology, 'since reason cannot be either exclusively secular or entirely natural'. "For reason itself, whether it knows it or not, only derives its power of knowing from the liberality of a God who is the 'Father of lights' (James 1:17), and from a Word who is the 'True Light which, coming into the world, enlightens every man' (John 1:9)."[14] "Only the

12 Ibid., 106.
13 Ibid., 59.
14 Ibid., 61.

grace of an illumination coming from God can give to man the desire and capacity to ascend towards Him."[15] "To the incompleteness of reason — there is no pure nature"[16] — corresponds "its natural demand for a supernatural completion in the intellective and even supra-intellective order"; intelligence "is supranatural by nature," "its essence is metaphysical"; "the intellect (*nous*) is already something divine."[17]

This is why there is, at the end of theology as at its beginning, that by which, "in a manner surpassing speech and knowledge, we reach a union superior to anything available to us by way of our own abilities or activities in the realm of discourse or of intellect."[18]

THE PSYCHIC AND THE SPIRITUAL

Borella's Lumières de la théologie mystique *has in this way distinguished intelligence and reason. From this same work we shall draw the initial article below: "The natural need of reason for an intellective, supernatural completion." But in* Amour et vérité *we will more particularly find an anthropological presentation; this will be the next article: "Reason-submissiveness and intellect-intuition," followed by a third, drawn from* The Crisis of Religious Symbolism: *"Principles constitute the nature of intelligence."*

Of course, this fundamental distinction between intelligence and reason is not without links to another, no less fundamental one, that between the psychic and the spiritual. In order to deal with this distinction without going too much into the anthropological doctrine of human tripartition (body, soul, spirit), the Christian doctrine of the 'pneumatization of the intellect',[19] as presented in Amour et vérité, *will indirectly illustrate this in a fourth article.*

15 Dionysius the Areopagite, *Heavenly Hierarchy*, 120B–121A. Cf. Borella, *Lumières de la théologie mystique*, 61.

16 "The idea that reason is entirely natural and completely autonomous (and therefore self-sufficient) in its own order seems far . . . from the truth" (Borella, *Lumières de la théologie mystique*, 92).

17 Ibid., 92–3. 'The Spirit is one with the Father, and the Son, *and ours*', says St. Augustine (*De Trinitate*, V, 14).

18 Dionysius the Areopagite, *Divine Names*, 585B–588A. Cf. *Lumières de la théologie mystique*, 87.

19 From the ancient Greek *pneuma*: breath.

The Natural Need of Reason for an Intellective Supernatural Completion

To suppose, as neo-Thomism does, that there exists "an entirely natural and perfectly autonomous (i.e., self-sufficient) reason, derives from the adoption of too schematic an Aristotelianism, which indeed conceals a fundamentally naturalist tendency." Its effects (not entirely neutralized by scholastic theology) have been the anti-intellectualist reaction of affective mysticism as well as the powerful Lutherian revolt. "To the contrary, Denys teaches, with Plato, the heteronomy and incompleteness of reason (there is no pure nature) and its natural demand for an intellective supernatural completion, even a supra-intellective or supra-noetic one."[20] The scholastic adage '*Gratia non tollit naturam sed perficit*' (grace does not suppress nature but perfects it) means:

- "on one hand, an incompleteness of reason, and therefore some heteronomy, in its merely human state and in its own activity, as well as a conscious need for a transcendent illumination able to transform this reason into spiritual intelligence, and so, to really change it into itself";
- on the other, it requires a spiritual and quasi-supernatural capacity to receive this gnostic illumination and be deified by it.

In this perspective, intelligence is both less and more than what 'scholastic philosophism' conceives, because it is supernatural by nature: "for St. Thomas . . . 'the whole of the divine mystery is already present in the very nature of the intellect',[21] just as for Denys and the Platonists the intellect (*nous*) is already something divine (*theios*)."[22]

Reason-Submissiveness and Intellect-Intuition

One's mental state is the cognitive modality of the psychism. The mirror seems a good descriptive image inasmuch as the "specific nature of such

20 *Lumières de la théologie mystique*, 92. Emphasis added.
21 *Letters of Étienne Gilson to Henri de Lubac* (San Francisco: Ignatius, 1988), 95; *Lumières de la théologie mystique*, 93.
22 Roques, *Structures théologiques. De la gnose à Richard de Saint-Victor* (Paris: P.U.F., 1962), 166. Also: Dionysius 1193 A 343; *Lumières de la théologie mystique*, 93.

knowledge is its indirect character": our mentality thinks about or 'reflects' on what it knows.[23] It does not penetrate the object through to its essence, but it is the object that 'penetrates' into it as an abstraction. Admittedly, what is known is the object, not the abstraction, "but this object is known by mode of abstraction . . . our mentality is the 'refracting medium' through which the object passes in order to become known."[24]

This knowledge by indirect or reflected 'mental impression' thus introduces what Ruyer terms a 'psychic distance' between man and the world.[25] From then on, "the *conceptible* [the conceptible is to reason what the intelligible is to intelligence] exists thus not only in things but also in a way in itself, since human knowledge actualizes, in a separated state, the intelligible modality of things." All the more so because, and this is what distinguishes man from animals, this is not so much a matter of thinking or expressing something, but of thinking *about* something or speaking *about* something. Since this has to do with something 'absent', "one sees that mental knowledge not only implies conceptual thinking but also memory and imagination, functions of absence in time and space."[26]

"Mental knowledge not only receives and elaborates 'impressions', it organizes them among themselves, connecting them according to the set relationships imposed as rules on our mental world. All these rules constitute the proper architecture of the mind: this is reason! [. . .] In this activity, our mental state remains, if not passive, at least subdued. Indeed, and this is a very important point, the rational structure of the mind appears, to the mind itself, as if it were an inexplicable 'foreign' presence."[27] As such, our mentality is situated between two demands:

- the object towards which it turns: the internal or external world imposed on it,
- but also its own internal structure, reason: the coherent whole of logical principles that governs all human knowledge.

23 'Think' and 'reflect' can be a single verb in French: 'réfléchir'.
24 *Amour et vérité* (Paris: l'Harmattan, 2011), 108–9. English trans.: *Love and Truth: The Christian Path of Charity* forthcoming from Angelico Press, 2018.
25 Cf. Raymond Ruyer, *L'Animal, l'Homme et la Fonction symbolique* (Paris: Gallimard, 1964); *Amour et vérité*, 109.
26 *Amour et vérité*, 109.
27 Ibid., 110.

These two "demands are imposed on it with equal authority," indeed they are two 'objectivities': one the objectivity of things (even if only for the psychism) and the other that of logical relations. Hence we have this dual obedience of the mind, its "submission to logical principles as well as to the nature of things."[28]

This mental knowledge, subject to reason and to its 'impressions', goes "from the world to reason, and from reason to the world." Where they meet is in the concept: the means or mediator of this knowledge, which can be called discursive (discursiveness being a path subject to duality, division). Actually, it is not knowledge itself that is discursive, but the process of perpetual confrontation between the respective demands of things and those of reason; knowledge itself is sheer intuition, 'vision' (or 'hearing'), the direct and unifying perception of its object.

"That knowledge is intuitive, and not the conclusion of some reasoning process, is clear. . . . It is primary, irreducible, and ungenerated." The process of acquiring knowledge (and of establishing its validity) is not intuitive: in order to discover what is not known, the mind proceeds discursively, using inquiry, reasoning, and deduction. But the proper act of knowing can only be the "direct reception of intelligible data." The cognitive act, as such, is that by which "a known object is directly united with a knowing subject in a kind of mutual transparency. This is the very experience of the intelligible."[29]

And yet his distinction between the reason (*dianoia, ratio*) and the intellect (*nous, intellectus*) is not a "total separation, for *ratio* is the broken and fragmentary light of *intellectus*. But they should not be confused, nor should we deny either of these modes of cognitive activity."[30]

Surprisingly enough, though, such a confusion occurs in Descartes' philosophy, as exemplified in his second *Meditation*, where *ratio* and *intellectus* are said to be equivalent, while "prior philosophic tradition almost constantly had distinguished them."[31]

As a logical consequence of this Cartesian confusion, next we come to the negation of *intellectus* (intuitive intellect) in the work of Kantian philosophy. "Endeavoring to assume a critical consciousness of reason (*The Critique of Pure Reason*), Kant did not perceive the power with which the Cartesian

28 Ibid., 123.
29 Ibid., 111.
30 Idid., 113.
31 Ibid., 112–13.

confusion still endowed intuitive knowledge (*intellectus intuitivus*). Without *intellectus*, no metaphysic is possible: 'Intellectual intuition . . . is not ours, and [its] possibility . . . is precluded from our insight.'"[32]

Making reason (*Vernunft*) the superior faculty of knowing, "Kant is led to reverse what the whole prior philosophic tradition had accepted and to call understanding (*Verstand, intellectus*) the inferior cognitive activity, i.e., the one that invests sensible knowledge with some conceptual or mental form."

"From an initial confusion to negationist inversion: this is the way followed by Western intellectual decadence."[33]

We will conclude with the paradox of the intellect:

> The intellect can receive into itself the knowledge of everything only because it is none of the things it knows. . . . [T]his intellect indeed merits the name 'speculative intellect' because it is a mirror (*speculum* in Latin) that reflects the world. The price to be paid for its lucidity is a kind of distancing from reality, thanks to which reality as such is revealed to man, but also by which man is set apart from being in his very being. Knowledge is clearly an intelligible communion of the knowing and the known, but this is in some manner a communion at a distance. With cognitive activity, everything transpires as if man had retained the memory of an ontological communion between himself and the world, but he can achieve this — by his merely natural powers — only in speculative mode. Knowledge is this very possibility, this ultimate possibility, this memory of a lost paradise. It is an anticipated fusion of subject and object, but anticipated only because unrealized.[34]

Principles Constitute the Nature of Intelligence

The principles of reason (such as the initial one, the non-contradiction principle) are so obvious that they reveal themselves only when contradictory

32 *The Critique of Pure Reason*, trans. W. Schwarz (Aalen: Scientia, 1982), 98; *Amour et vérité*, 113.

33 *Amour et vérité*, 113.

34 Ibid., 117.

consequences show they have been missed. They cannot be demonstrated—if so they would no longer be principles—but they constitute an internal requirement for reason. And reason agrees to this requirement "through a real intellectual intuition, the necessity for which is rightly irrefutable." These principles are thus "metalogical, or metarational, in the sense that logic and reason designate the order of a purely discursive knowledge, that is, a purely mediate (and therefore demonstrable) knowledge." They can be discovered, in their truly metalogical nature, only by a philosophy that transcends logic (without contradicting it). Therefore:

- "Logic is nothing but the sum-total of intellectual operations by which the human mind subordinates itself to principles in its cognitive activity."
- "Philosophy is not subordinate to principles, . . . they are deemed connatural to it; . . . intelligence knows them implicitly when knowing itself."[35]

This is why we should not consider these natural structures of the intelligence in the way Kant does, as if they were an *a priori* condition of the intellect. They are, to the contrary, perfectly transparent to it; "they are the intelligence itself, they are the *Logos*." For what belongs to the order of the intelligence is necessarily *sense*, *Logos*. The intellect cannot speak of unintelligible principles which it would obey without understanding, nor can it just decide that its understanding of them is pure illusion.

"Principles are clearly then the reflection of the intellect's structures in objective knowledge, granted, but these principles are also those of the *Logos* in itself, necessary and purely intelligible, for that is the sole proposition that the intellect can intelligibly hold—which implies that there is no *essential* heterogeneity between our intellect and the *Logos*."[36]

35 *The Crisis of Religious Symbolism*, 316.
36 Ibid., 317.

The Pneumatization of the Intellect [37]

We have seen above that the paradox of the intellect consists in this: "The intellect can receive into itself the knowledge of everything only because it is none of the things it knows"; and, likewise, if it can be the anticipated fusion of subject and object, this is because it does not bring about the fusion.

To bring about such a fusion, a true 'pneumatization of the intellect'[38] is necessary; failing that the intellect is only the cognitive aspect of the spirit, and, even if the intellect and the spirit are essentially identical, ordinary experience is just that of the intellect alone. To the contrary, a true 'pneumatization of the intellect' reveals the connaturality or *essential* identity of *intellectus* and *spiritus*, as shown for example by Meister Eckhart.[39]

It seems useful to briefly review here the human threefold constitution, clearly affirmed by St. Paul: "... may your whole spirit [*pneuma*] and soul [*psyche*] and body [*soma*] be kept blameless at the coming of our Lord Jesus Christ."[40] Moreover, the distinction between psychic and spiritual (or pneumatic, or celestial) bodies can be seen in the opposition between the first and the last Adam: "It is sown a natural body, it is raised a spiritual body. . . . The first man Adam became a living being [*psyche*]; the last Adam became a life-giving spirit [*pneuma*]. But it is not the pneumatic [spiritual] that is first but the natural, and then the pneumatic [spiritual]. The first man was from the earth, a man of dust; the second man is from heaven."[41]

To this opposition corresponds an alchemic spiritual rule: "The grace of the incarnate Word separates the pure gold of the spirit from its lethal alloy with psychic substances"[42] — a rule taught by St. Paul in his epistle to the Hebrews: "For the word [*Logos*] of God is living and active, sharper than any two-edged sword, piercing to the division of soul and of spirit, of joints and of marrow, and discerning the thoughts and intentions of the heart."[43] This means that "*pneuma* is actualized in ourselves only through *metanoia*, an inner

---

37 This doctrine is explained in *Amour et vérité*, 116–17, 143–45, 335–36, 343, 346–52.
38 From *pneuma* = spirit.
39 *Amour et vérité*, 116.
40 1 Thess. 5:23.
41 1 Cor. 15:47.
42 *Amour et vérité*, 142.
43 Heb. 4:12.

conversion, which is the purification of the *psyche* and the death of the *ego*." This conversion is but the human dimension of the transforming activity of divine grace; this is why the "Pauline *pneuma* is sometimes the Holy Spirit and sometimes the spiritual man, without it always being possible to discern which one is involved." This is because the originally 'inspired' (Gen. 2:17) spirit of man is still "indwelt by the Spirit of God that renews him (Eph. 4:23) and unites with him" (Rom. 8:16), so that "he who is united to the Lord becomes one *pneuma* with him" (1 Cor. 6:17).[44]

But what about links between the spirit (*pneuma*) and the intellect (*nous*), taking into account that St. Paul sometimes uses *pneuma* as a synonym for *nous*?[45] Once vocabulary variations are admitted, and according to our anthropology, one can say that:

- Spirit designates the divine life in the creature according to its innermost dimension, whose actualization depends strictly on the grace of Christ;
- Intellect designates the knowing faculty, which is 'naturally supernatural', and knows (or can know) the spiritual truth, but which, being 'passive' (by definition) — this is the price of its objectivity — is powerless to move the will of the being as a whole.

A capacity for pure knowledge (not abolished, but only obscured by original sin), the intellect enables the human being, in his present state, to *intelligibly* make contact with realities that *ontologically* surpass him; in other words, to have a clear consciousness of them: this is because the intellect is naturally supernatural, that is, supernatural realities make sense to a natural being; otherwise they would remain as if they were nonexistent. From this results a dual connection between *nous* and *pneuma*:

- This dual connection requires, first, an *intellectualization* of the spiritual, so that the Spirit's mysteries are actually 'understood';

---

44 *Amour et vérité*, 143–44.

45 Father Prat, *Theology of St. Paul*, trans. J. L. Stoddard (Westminster: Newman Bookshop, 1952), vol. 2, 54, note 4; *Amour et vérité*, 143.

- and, second, a pneumatization of the intellect, so as to give life and reality to what is only speculative and thus impotent knowledge.

The intellectualization of the *pneuma* is not only about the fruits of an 'understanding' of the mysteries, as in St. Paul's teaching: "For if I pray in a tongue, my spirit prays but my intellect [*nous*] is unfruitful. What am I to do? I will pray with the spirit and I will pray with the intellect also"; [46] it is also about instructing others: "I would rather speak five words with my mind in order to instruct others, than ten thousand words in a tongue."[47] However, although the intellect is the true 'hermeneut' of the spiritual, it remains powerless to enable us to enter the life of the spirit.

It is the pneumatization of the intellect that transforms the speculative intellect into the operative intellect:

- "Be transformed by the renewal of your mind, that by testing you may discern what is the will of God."[48]
- " . . . put off. . . the old man which grows corrupt according to the deceitful lusts and be renewed in the spirit [*pneuma*] of your mind, and . . . put on the new Man which was created according to God (*kata Theon*)."[49]
- "Who has known the Intellect of the Lord?" asks Isaiah.[50] And St. Paul's answer: "The pneumatic man judges all things; but is himself to be judged by no one. For who has known the intellect of the Lord so as to instruct him? But we have the intellect of Christ."[51]

"The goal of the pneumatization of the intellect is access to the inward Man, to the immortal Person" because "the intellect, in its true nature, is identical to the inward Man" and following St Paul:

---

46 1 Cor. 14:14–15.

47 1 Cor. 14:19. 'Words in a tongue' refers to a charismatic phenomenon that consists in the utterance of unintelligible words; *Amour et vérité*, 144.

48 *Rom.* 12:1–2. 'Transform' translates the *metamorphoó* of the Greek text.

49 *Eph.* 4:19–24.

50 This Isaian question (40:13) is quoted by St. Paul in Rom. 11:33; cf. *Amour et vérité*, 145, note 3.

51 1 Cor. 2:15–16.

- "I delight in the law of God, according to the inward man. . . . So then, I of myself serve the law of God with my intellect" (Rom. 7:22–25). "And you will receive the power to understand, along with all the saints, the Width, the Length, the Height and the Depth; you will know the Love of Christ that surpasses all knowledge" (Eph. 3:14–19).[52]

Such a knowledge that surpasses all knowledge is called gnosis (or mystical theology). Gnosis is therefore a holy knowledge, both by its object that is the Divine Essence and by its mode which is a sharing in the knowledge that God has of Himself. Such a sharing—derived more from being than from knowing—is an actualization that is necessarily the work of the Holy Spirit.

This actualization is the internal basis for holy theology just as Revelation is its external basis. With this dual basis, speculative theology is the mental objectification of mystical theology, an imperfect expression of perfect contemplation.

This very imperfection of speculative theology will lead to its being superseded, inviting reason to subject itself to spiritual intelligence and giving access, by grace, to gnosis. And this gnosis is the Kingdom of God, as underscored by the Gospel parallel between 'the key of gnosis'[53] and the 'key of the Kingdom of God',[54] the scriptural basis for the identity of gnosis and the Kingdom of God.

With this in mind we can say that true gnosis is not a science but a nescience, not a knowing but an unknowing. Indeed, in this supreme gnosis, as soon as the intellect is perfectly stripped of its own self, it is God who knows Himself. Only unknowing can lead to a surpassing of knowledge: "If any one imagines that he knows something, he does not yet know as he ought to know."[55] And the power that can achieve this necessary renunciation is the power of charity that leads us to say that "charity is the doorway to gnosis."[56]

According to Christ's prayer, we have to become one just as the Father and the Son are One. And Love is the unification that precedes Unity, because

---

52 *Amour et vérité*, 143–47.
53 Luke 11:52.
54 Matt. 23:13.
55 1 Cor. 8:1–2.
56 St. Evagrius of Pontus, *Letter to Anatolios*, P.G., t. XL, col. 1221 C; cf. *Amour et vérité*, 344.

love is the substance of gnosis, and gnosis the essence of love. The gnostic dimension of charity affords a completely disinterested pure love and a gnosis centered on Truth, the only one that gives freedom. "Gnosis is the immutable and invisible vertical axis which the dance of love envelops like a flame."[57]

That is why prayer is the only activity consonant with the dignity of the intellect. It is the only means for the intellect to achieve its deiform nature. Prayer is therefore gnosis; "it is the intellect that prays in knowledge and knows in prayer";[58] knowledge is the prayer of the Intellect. Prayer and gnosis are as such the two uprights of Jacob's ladder that meet in God's infinity.

If we admit stages on this spiritual ladder, they are the different stages of renouncing in turn the desires of the body, the passions of the soul, and the thoughts of the spirit. Thus the (somatic) virtues of the body can lead by grace to the (psychic) virtues of the soul, the virtues of the soul to the (pneumatic) virtues of the spirit, and the virtues of the spirit to essential gnosis.

Love and Gnosis are both the beginning and end of the journey. Having reached Christ, the eternal Father's gnosis, through charity, we partake of His Effusion of Love that is the Holy Spirit. The intellect, unified by charity, is "raised to an infinite dignity, a dignity that it possesses by very virtue of its intellectual nature." And "the naked intellect is the one that is consumed in the vision of itself and has merited communion with the contemplation of the Holy Trinity."[59]

"The nakedness of the intellect, or infinite ignorance [St. Evagrius], and the cloud of unknowing [St. Dionysius] represent the non-modal way by which the creature can become immanent to divine transcendence." And "this non-modal way is charity's highest degree."

"As long as the intellect is not God, its light is not the true Light." It has to realize its own non-divine substance, that is, its ontological ignorance. "The Blessed Virgin knew this secret, she who was the pure darkness where the Light of the world took flesh."[60]

57 *Amour et vérité*, 343.
58 St. Evagrius of Pontus, *Centuries*, IV, 43; cf. *Amour et vérité*, 345.
59 Cf. Père Hausherr, *Les leçons d'un contemplatif*; *Amour et vérité*, 352.
60 *Amour et vérité*, 354.

TWO

Esoterism and Gnosis

ESOTERICISM, METAPHYSICS, AND GNOSIS

In his Christ the Original Mystery, *Jean Borella had to address three questions: first, to show that, despite its fundamental contribution to the codification of esotericism, the definition of esotericism given by Guénon was somehow self-limited; second, to show how those limits lead to the impossibility of applying this definition to all cases, especially in the case of Christianity; and third, to show Christianity in its own light, that is, free from Guénonian patterns, in order to unveil its very own essence.*

The first part of the book, dealing with the limitations of the Guénonian approach to esotericism, was therefore the ideal place to address esotericism, more precisely compared to metaphysics and real gnosis.[1]

From Ancient to Modern 'Esotericism': A Forced Definition

Although the adjective 'esoteric' has always existed (at least since the Aristotelian circles of the first century AD), the origins of the noun 'esotericism' are both recent and dubious. It arose within the milieu of "a socialistic romanticism that will inspire the Revolution of 1848." This was "a nebulous ideology in which the religion of Humanity and the cult of democracy are combined with confused speculations on the Trinity, women, and progress (both industrial and social)."[2]

---

1 *Christ the Original Mystery: Esoterism and the Mystical Way* (Brooklyn, NY: Angelico Press/Sophia Perennis, 2018), first part: "Nature of the Esoteric Perspective," 13–85. The first part of Jean Borella's work on this subject was edited by Bruno Bérard in *Introduction to the Metaphysics of the Christian Mysteries (In the light of its ancient and modern commentators with regards to the Buddhist, Hindu, Islamic, Jewish and Taoist traditions)* [in French], imprimatur (Paris: l'Harmattan, 2005).

2 *Christ the Original Mystery*, 16.

Even if part of this initial sentimentalism remains in the marvels of the pseudo-sciences and in current New-Age animism, the unifying concept of esotericism has achieved in the meantime the status of a universal category of philosophical and religious thought. Nevertheless, this status has assumed such an importance that we are led to ask how our civilizations have managed to do without such a fundamental notion for so many centuries!

In short, this switch from adjective to noun (apart from all the excesses unfortunately denoted by this noun) reveals above all the loss of an intuitive knowledge — "How beautiful!" — for the sake of a search for the safety of a rational knowledge: "What is beauty?" But once the question is asked, we then have to try to give an answer. In this case the answer will have to be the definition of esotericism, a noun we cannot do without anymore, or so it would seem.

Back to Etymological Roots: Three Indications for a Clear Definition

The Greek adjective *esoterikos* gives us three indications. *Eso* (or *eiso*) means 'inside', with a sense of movement : 'to go to the inside'; *ter* (from *teros*) indicates a comparison: 'more to the inside (than)'; and the ending *-ikos* signifies 'that which has as particular nature to go more to the inside (than)'. Therefore, we have here three notions:

- The notion of 'inside' is obvious; this means passing beyond external appearances.
- The notion of movement to the inside is less known. This means that esotericism cannot be still but is the necessary and continual movement further inward. Thus there is neither institutional esotericism nor any esoteric institution as such.
- As for the notion of comparison, this of course refers to the *relative*[3] opposition between esotericism and exotericism.[4] This means that there can be no esotericism without exotericism. Just as there can be no absolute exotericism, so there can be no absolute esotericism

---

3 Distinct from other types of opposition, 'father-son' is a classic example of relative opposition.

4 We find this opposition in Saint Clement of Alexandria: *Stromata*, V, 9; *P.G.* IX, col. 90 (cf. *Histoire et théorie du symbole* [Lausanne: L'Age d'Homme, 2004], 40, note 20).

pure and free from all shape and revelation (as Hegel, for instance, would have wished).

Esotericism is therefore an approach that always leads (movement) further (relative opposition) behind mere appearances (inside).

The Relative Opposition between Exotericism and Esotericism puts them on the same Hermeneutic Level

However superior esotericism might be to exotericism, both remain, first, on the same side of knowledge and, second, on the same side of the sacred-profane boundary.

- First of all, esotericism and exotericism obviously both stem from the field of the 'sacred' with its distinction from the 'profane' — a distinction still visible today, if we compare the architecture of a building for everyday use to a cathedral or a Gregorian chant to a popular song.
- Secondly, if gnosis realizes an identity between knowing, known and knowledge, exotericism and esotericism are only related to the course that possibly leads to it. They are therefore both related to the general category of hermeneutics: the art of interpretation, of explanation.

Besides, we can find in the Scriptures the roots of this multi-storey hermeneutic, where different comprehension levels of the mysteries co-exist in a natural way:

- "To you has been given the secret of the kingdom of God, but for those outside everything is in parables so that they may indeed see but not perceive."[5]
- "Is a lamp brought in to be put under a basket, or under a bed? ... For nothing is hidden except to be made manifest; nor is anything secret except to come to light."[6]

5 Mark 4:11–12.
6 Mark 4:21–22.

- "With many such parables he spoke the word to them, as they were able to hear it."[7]

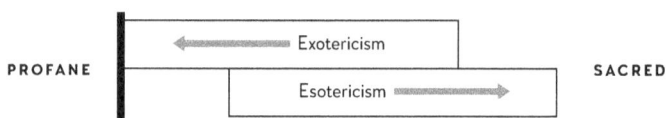

The Relative Opposition between Exotericism and Esotericism calls for their Complement: the *Revelatum*

If esotericism and exotericism are hermeneutic intentions more or less imbued with a deep sense of tradition, this is the proof that they both call for a revelation to interpret, to understand, to comment upon. And this revelation is, alone, the expression of the divine truth in the human world. This *revelatum* is itself unique, ontological and transcendental.

Thus, beyond the relative opposition between exotericism and esotericism, we encounter above all a triple opposition between:

- The multiplicity of forms (exotericism) and interpretations (esotericism) versus the unicity of a revelation;
- The intellectual-spiritual nature of any hermeneutic experience opposed to the objective being of the *revelatum*; in this way, we can see in gnosis, which surpasses any hermeneutic perspective whatsoever, the leap into ontological realization;
- And our creaturely horizontality (as esoteric as the approach might be) confronted with transcendental verticality.

In concrete terms, all of the above confirms that there can be no absolute or institutionalized esotericism — which would not be in motion anymore, even if some specific institutions show some particularly esoteric (Taoism and Sufism) or exoteric (Confucianism) trend. So, even though the essence of esotericism is the search for the essential and goes beyond the revealed form as such, this does not however mean that there should be either an essential esotericism or an essential religion.[8]

---

7 Mark 4:33–34.
8 *Christ the Original Mystery,* 36–37.

This also means that exotericism and esotericism both contemplate the same mysteries. Only their interpretation will be either esoteric or exoteric. In Christianity, for instance, although the metaphysical interpretation of Redemption is more esoteric than a very exoteric moral interpretation, it is definitely the same unique mystery that inspires them both.

Although there is no Universal Esotericism, yet Esotericism is, as a Spiritual Approach, Something Universal

Clearly an approach that consists in getting closer and closer to the inner mystery of revelation cannot be considered as a unique universal esotericism. However, because we can pass beyond each type of revelation—pass beyond its letter, not its content—each revelation will have its own specific esotericism. If we admit that this approach is found in all religions, we can therefore say that esotericism is universal.

In Hinduism, there is the central revelation, the *Veda*, unique and immutable, and the six *darshana* (*nyaya* and *vaisheshika, yoga* and *sankhya, mimamsa* and *vedanta*), which are precisely the points of view that enable one to get close to it.

In Islam, we likewise have these distinctions:

- The *shariyah*, the external, the exoteric religious law, literally the 'great way', that can be represented by a circumference in motion, in relation with the *cosmic wheel*;
- the *haqiqah*, the truth or essential reality that is (re)presented as the immutable and immobile center of this cosmic wheel, its principial unity, the pure gnosis where metaphysical revelation happens; and
- the *tariqah*, the 'path' or the narrow way which leads from the circumference to the center. This path towards the inside is literally esotericism.[9]

Even so, this static Guénonian diagram of circle and radius remains in line with Guénon's 'two-sided' conception that "can lead to a reinforcement of the

9 René Guénon, *Insights into Islamic Esoterism and Taoism* (Hillsdale, NY: Sophia Perennis, 2004), 10, n. 5; *Christ the Original Mystery*, 56.

opposition between exotericism and esotericism" in such a way that both hermeneutic modes end up being "entitatively posited in their pure and exclusive reality,
and we see conferred on them the nature of an objective, nearly autonomous
form, a form perfectly definable institutionally and surveyable." In reality, those
two modes are, one like the other, both referring to the unique *revelatum*, and
it is clearly at the summit of a perpendicular transecting a circle's center that
we should ultimately 'locate' this *haqîqah*. Furthermore, the dynamic synthesis
of radius and circumference in the shape of a concentric spiral would better
express "that exotericism and esotericism are hermeneutic *operations*, 'wayfarings'
and living pathways and not fixed geometric determinations . . . inadequate
for getting a clear idea of the spiritual life, which is both circular and radial."[10]

From Esoteric Veiling to Metaphysical Unveiling[11]

Anything unveiled is never entirely so because its invisible root, its cause and
source, will never be unveiled. In this case we can say that esotericism reveals
that a portion is not-unveiled and therefore there is a veiling.

Quite different is pure metaphysical theory; its language, composed of the
most abstract concepts and principles and of the most logical sequences, is
more transparent. Indeed, insofar as metaphysics uses the very language of the
intelligence, the intellective act becomes one with intelligence itself. In this
way, metaphysical discourse operates at the very limit of ultimate hermeneutics; it is the last interpreter and cannot be interpreted in its turn. Moreover,
in its ultimate positioning, the language of metaphysics can only indicate its
esoteric superseding by suggesting its own elimination with a non-formal but
real apophasis that would put in motion its own 'self-obliteration'.[12] "Blessed
are the intelligences that can close their eyes,"[13] as Dionysius the Areopagite
has already indicated.

Nevertheless, as a complement to the intellectual mode, metaphysics can
also use the symbolic mode; both modes "are essential: the symbolic mode

---

10   *Christ the Original Mystery*, 55–57. See below, Chapter 3, "The four ways of theology."
11   Ibid., 62–70.
12   Guy Bugault, *Les Etudes philosophiques*, October–December 1983, 400; *Christ the
Original Mystery*, 65.
13   *Mystical Theology* I, 1; following Gandillac's French translation in *Œuvres complètes*
(Paris: Aubier, 1943), 177.

makes us see and the intellective mode makes us understand."[14] However, this does not change the position of metaphysics as the ultimate esotericism (without any further interpretation possible), and, by this very fact, the hermeneutic the most ontologically dependent on its object, which is the sole interpreted material with which it is preoccupied: the *revelatum*. As far as the symbol, which can also be seen as a visible 'interpreter' of an invisible 'interpreted', is concerned, it also depends on what it interprets, but insofar as it is ontologically united with what is presentified within it.

But since the intellect speaks its own language, a language that is natural, it will even deal naturally with supernatural things. And yet, if it is 'at home' in both natural and supernatural realms, this is also because it is naturally nowhere — 'The intellect comes through the door' or 'from without', says Aristotle.[15] That is why, once again, we are led to that death of speech necessarily required by true metaphysics. However, to this *sacrificium intellectus*, to this deliberate annihilation of the intellect itself, to this ultimate renunciation corresponds a resurrection. To the renunciation of the vanity of our own light corresponds the entrance into the 'more than luminous darkness' (St. Dionysius the Areopagite): true gnosis.

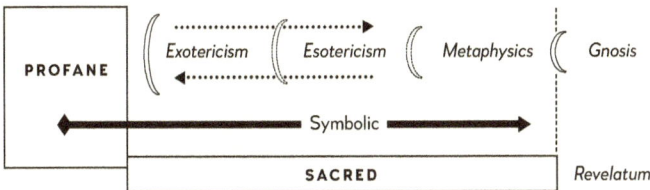

GNOSIS AND GNOSTICISMS

Complementing this gradation — we have progressively made distinctions between the profane and the sacred, then exotericism and esotericism, and finally metaphysics and gnosis — it would be interesting to contrast now, in a pedagogic way, gnosis and gnosticism. As it happens, 'gnosticism' is a category created by historians of religion, while 'gnosis' — although its origins lie in Scripture — was denounced, even in Christian spheres, as the worst corruption of

---

14 *Christ the Original Mystery*, 68.
15 *On the Generation of Animals*, II.3, 736 A27–B12; *Christ the Original Mystery*, 69.

Faith! It is even more necessary to clarify this paradox of gnosis in Christianity since we want to establish it as fundamentally Christian! Indeed gnosis — saving inner knowledge — is perfectly applicable to the message of Christ:[16] *"And this is eternal life, that they know you the only true God, and Jesus Christ whom you have sent" (John 17:3).*

That Christianity is a gnostic religion and even real gnosis[17] *is clearly what Jean Borella wanted to remind us of and explain. He has done this in a number of articles, three of which — reprinted in* Problèmes de gnose *(Paris: l'Harmattan, 2007) — are especially instructive in this regard and, for the most part, are summed up here.*[18]

Historical, Historiographical and Scriptural Sources

A religious or philosophical doctrine can also be defined from an historical (who, where, when) or speculative (what) angle. In the case of gnosticism, its history is above all its historiography, known only through its refutation carried out by its Christian opponents (and neo-Platonists): the second- and third-century heresiologists, such as St. Irenaeus, St. Justin, and St. Hippolytus. Their citations of long, often gnostic, texts were the basis for the documentation used by historians from the eighteenth to the twentieth century. Even though the discovery of the Nag-Hammadi (Upper-Egypt) gnostic library (probably dating from the fourth century) in 1945 considerably increased the number of documents available, it still left a number of questions unanswered.

The historians' succession of theses (after Henri-Charles Puech and Jean Doresse) brought to light how difficult it can be to situate a derivation (gnosticism) without being always able to situate the thing itself (gnosis):

16 *Problèmes de gnose* (Paris: l'Harmattan, 2007), 20.

17 Ibid., 44.

18 "Gnose chrétienne et gnoses anti-chrétiennes" (15–29), "La gnose au vrai nom" (45–74) — translated in *The Secret of the Christian Way* (Albany, NY: SUNY Press, 2001), 5–27, 182–8 — and "Gnose et gnosticisme chez René Guénon" in *Dossier H: René Guénon* (Lausanne: L'Age d'Homme, 1984), 143–221. Finally, a summary of these studies is included in the conversation with Éric Vatré entitled "Intelligence spirituelle et surnaturel" in *La droite du Père* (Paris: Guy Trédaniel, 1994), extracts of which are used in this book. Another vision of Gnosis, "The Pneumatization of the Intellect," will be found in *Amour et vérité*, 144–7, as referenced above.

- Gnosticism was first seen as a purely Christian heresy and was therefore dated from the first and second centuries. For some (like Harnack) it consisted of a 'premature radical Hellenization' of an oriental religion and, for some others (such as Bousset), of a regression towards its oriental origins of a religion initially of a Greek type.

- It then became obvious that some trends characterized as gnostic existed before Christianity, namely Jewish apocalyptic (dating from the first century BC), the Mandean religious group and some Iranian (Manichean) and Egyptian (hermetist) groups.

The possibility of these two contradictory theses allows us to bring a third one forward: "Christianity is a gnostic religion. It is real gnosis, gnosis in all its purity." Having said this, we can understand that some pre-Christian gnostics saw in Christian revelation their own vision of the Divine and wanted to use it for their own benefit. We can also understand how many historians were not able to see in gnosticism anything else than a properly Christian heresy. If gnosticism seems so Christian, seeing that many schools of thought can be associated with it, this is proof that Christianity is a genuine Gnosis.[19]

So much so that, without denying the fact of a religious Hellenism or of an Egyptian tradition — two sources that historians wanted to attribute to biblical *gnosis* — we have to admit that, by itself, the concept of 'influence' appealed to by historians inevitably leads to the concept of 'sources'. Now, even if there can be influences from one tradition to another leading to the transfer of peripheral elements, this should not be applied to what is most essential in all these traditions.

Although we can spot some 'clearly metaphysical' usages of the word *gnosis* as early as Plato (cf. *Politicus* 258e), in the opposition within the *episteme* between what is related to practice — *he praktike* — and what is referred to as 'gnostic' — *he gnostike* (that is to say pure and speculative knowledge) — it is the Greek-speaking Jewish (scriptural and liturgical) tradition that first uses *gnosis* in religious terms, by way of the verb *ginosko*, in order to translate the Hebrew *yd'*, "giving to the Greek word its full religious meaning":[20]

---

19 Cf. "Gnose chrétienne et gnose anti-chrétienne," op. cit.

20 Dom Jacques Duont, *Gnôsis. La connaissance religieuse dans les épttres de saint Paul* (Paris: Gabalda, Paris, 1949), 357–65; cf. *Problèmes de gnose*, 35 and note 20, same page.

"the revealed knowledge whose author is God or *Sophia*."[21] Besides, no
matter the influences that lead to the semantic specification of *gnosis*, we
have to admit that this word was far from being the only one available to
the Greek language. Indeed, Plato and Aristotle also used in a similar way
the nouns *epistème* (and the verbs *epistasthai* or *eidenai*), *dianoia*, *dianoesis*
(and *dianoesthai*), *gnome*, *logos*, *mathema*, *mathesis* (and *manthanei*), *noesis*
(and *noein*), *noema*, *nous*, *phronesis*, *sophia*, *sunesis*, etc. Nevertheless, the
Septuagint Bible is the only sacred text of pre-Christian antiquity to use
gnosis without the complement of a noun, when it almost always requires
one (knowledge *of* something) — which is not the case with *episteme*. This
means that *gnosis* refers to absolute knowledge, God's knowledge. And we
can admit, along with Rudolf Bultmann, that it is "not knowledge as a result
but rather the act of knowing."[22] God is thus "the God of gnosis," as we
read in 1 Samuel 2:3, and we find *gnosis* used fifteen times in this sense in the
book of Proverbs. The book of Wisdom also speaks of "God's gnosis."[23] But
this is not yet Gnosis in the way of a purely inner and deifying knowledge.
Gnosis is therefore "not only an action but also a state that only God can
give to the pneumatized intellect."[24] Gnosis defined as such is most often
mentioned in the New Testament, where it occurs twenty-nine times: twice
in St. Luke (1:77 — "the gnosis of salvation" — and 11:52), once in St. Peter
(1 Pet. 3:7 — the only occurrence of a non-religious meaning of the word)
and twenty-six times in St. Paul (especially 1 and 2 Corinthians, Colossians,
1 Timothy, Romans and Ephesians). Although the gnostic sense of the term,
the sense of a higher knowledge, is above all Paulinian (St. Paul also uses
epignosis), it is far from being absent in Saint Luke: "Woe to you lawyers! For
you have taken away the key of knowledge" (11:52) — all the more striking if
we admit that gnosis is the real key that can be identified with the 'Kingdom
of Heaven', as the parallel in St. Matthew (16:19) shows.

21 R. Bultmann, article on *ginosko* in *Theologisches Wörterbuch zum Neuen Testament* (Stutgart: Verlag W. Kohlhammer, 1966), tome I, 688–715, esp. 699; cf. *Problèmes
de gnose*, ibid.
22 *Theologisches Wörterbuch*, 689; cf. *Problèmes de gnose*, 34.
23 *The Secret of the Christian Way*, 182 note 3.
24 *Problèmes de gnose*, 36.

HELLENISTIC ANTIQUITY (PLATO)	JEWISH TRADITION & OLD TESTAMENT	NEW TESTAMENT
Metaphysic meaning	Religious Meaning	
Pure Knowledge	Unveiled Knowledge	Internal and Deifying Knowledge
'result'	'action'	'state'
Gnosis		

The whole of Christianity is in its essence a message of Gnosis: "Know and worship God in spirit and truth" (John 4:23 and 17:3), the union with Christ who is Himself the Gnosis of the Father. He is the incarnation of the Father's Gnosis, come to reopen the 'narrow door' of spiritual interiority, etc. We could even say: more than Christian, Gnosis is Christic by essence.[25]

Did you say "Gnostic"?

Gnosticism is a category elaborated by the historians of religions? Yes, this is true, since the heresiologists knew how to distinguish between a self- or otherwise-imposed label in their historiographical sources. This is the case with St. Irenaeus of Lyon, who mentions in his *Adversus Haereses,* for instance, that those he often refers to as 'gnostics' call themselves 'disciples' of Valentinus,[26] although he never identifies them in a clear and direct manner.[27] Elsewhere, St. Irenaeus clearly states — as do some other ecclesiastic writers — that the heretics he mentions, such as Carpocrates and the Carpocratians, 'give themselves the title of gnostic'.[28] St. Clement of Alexandria says the same of some disciples of a certain Prodicos[29] and the Carpocratians.[30] However, although both saints view the Carpocratians as 'licentious Gnostics', Irenaeus calls them Christianized Jews while Clement calls them Platonists![31] We can also mention St. Epiphanius, who clearly refuses to identify the Valesians (a sect of eunuchs) as 'gnostics'.[32]

---

25 "Gnose et gnosticisme chez René Guénon," 96–98.
26 St. Irenaeus, *Contre les hérésies (Against the Heresies)*, Préambule 2 (Paris: Cerf, 1984), 28.
27 Ibid., I, 29, 1 and note 1 of Father Adelin Rousseau, 121.
28 Ibid., I, 25, 6.
29 *Stromata*, III, 30; I, 69; VII, 41.
30 Ibid., III, 5, 1.
31 Cf. A Méhat, *Études sur les Stromates* (Seuil), 402–3.
32 *Panarion*, LVIII, 1, 3. *Panarion* ('Medicine Chest') is also known as *Haereses*.

Ultimately, we have to remember that Christian writers always name sects
and heresies after the name of their (supposed) founder: Nicolatians, Mar-
cionites, Valentinians, etc. Thanks to these few examples[33] we can see that it
is the heresiologists, the theologians, polemicists and ecclesiastic writers who
are in a position to describe a specific heresy, who provide historians with the
categories that can from then on be organized into subjects of study. Nothing
in this historiography gives us the possibility of describing gnosticism *in itself*.
What is more, among all the so-called gnostic sects, only the Ophites are clearly
designated by name.[34] We therefore have to restore the truth about gnosticism,
which can be summed up by the following statements:

- The word *Gnosticism* comes very late in French — 1842! It was first
  coined in English by the Cambridge Platonist Henry More (1614–
  1687), who used it 'in a pejorative sense';[35]
- the idea defined by the word, although earlier, does not go back
  farther than the seventeenth century;
- 'gnosticism', identified as one school of thought, even when exhibit-
  ing several forms but with enough in common to be included under
  one single concept and one single name, is unknown to the entirety
  of the medieval doctors and theologians;
- Christian antiquity is itself unaware of it: "In primitive Christianity
  there is no trace of 'gnosticism', in the sense of a vast historical category, and the modern use of 'gnostic' and 'gnosticism', designating
  a religious movement at once ample and poorly defined, is totally
  unknown in the first Christian era";[36]
- there is no school of thought that calls itself gnostic and is marked
  by a clearly defined doctrinal corpus;

---

33 Cf. the account in Michel Tardieu and Jean-Daniel Dubois, *Introduction à la
littérature gnostique* (Paris: Cerf, 1986), 26–29.

34 The Ophites (from the Greek *ophis* = snake), identified as Naaseans (from the
Hebrew *nahash* = snake), considered that the Genesis snake came to unveil to Adam the
true knowledge forbidden by the evil Creator (*Problèmes de gnose*, 33).

35 Roelof van den Broek, *Dictionary of Gnosis & Western Esotericism*, ed. Wouter J.
Hanegraaff (Leiden & Boston: Brill, 2006), 403–5.

36 R.P. Casey, "The Study of Gnosticism," in *The Journal of Theological Studies*,
num. 36, 1935, 55.

- finally, we cannot find any written records in the official texts of the
  ecclesiastical magisterium of any condemnation of a heresy named
  'gnosis' or 'gnosticism'.

Thus, the presence in a number of sects of the two most recurrent themes —
1) the condemnation of the Old Testament and its God, and 2) the rejection
of the sensible world — should not lead the historian to associate this category
of gnostic with the whole school of thought.

The variety of the so-called gnostic practices that we find described in many
authors' works[37] confirms that it is important to avoid falling into that trap.
Thus we read, for example, of parodies of the Eucharist involving the con-
sumption of sperm and menstrual blood.[38] But, in addition to these orgiastic
cults of 'Eucharistic cannibalism',[39] we should mention the apparition of the
'donkey-headed god' in a treatise that stems from 'gnostic' literature.[40] We
refer to the 'foul account' that says that Zachariah would have been killed in
the Temple because he told the Jews he saw, in the Holy of Holies, a man with
a donkey head. Thanks to Flavius Josephus we know that this calumny had
already been reported by Apion (a grammarian from Alexandria) during the
first century AD ("the Jews worship a golden donkey head").[41] Tacitus likewise
attributes donkey-worship to the Jews.[42] And Tertullian — in his *Defense of the
Christians against the Heathens* — reports, after having condemned Tacitus's
calumnies, that a painting exhibited in Rome showed the inscription *God of the
Christians engendered by a donkey* (*onokoites*)[43] and represented its subject with
donkey ears, hooves, and a book in hand, and dressed in a toga.[44] Egyptian in
origin (the god Set), this figure was accorded the name 'Typhon' by the Greeks;

37 For example, Saint Epiphanius, *Adversus Haereses*, lib. I, book II. Cf. also *Adversus
Haereses* XXVI, ch. IV and V; *P.G.*, t. XLI, col. 338–39.

38 *Secret of the Christian Way*, 14–15.

39 The expression is from Michel Tardieu.

40 St. Epiphanius, *Adversus Haereses*, lib. I, book II. Cf. also *Adversus Haereses* XXVI,
XII; *P.G.*, t. XLI, col. 349–51. Here he is speaking of the 'gnostic' book *Genna Marias*
(The Lineage of Mary).

41 *Against Apion*, Bk. II, 7, in *The Works of Flavius Josephus*, trans. Whiston, vol. IV
(Philadelphia: Lindsay & Blakiston, 1859), 419.

42 *Histories*, I. V, 3–4.

43 *Onokoites*, that is to say, issued from the coupling of a woman and a donkey.

44 *Apologétique*, XVI ; French trans. Nisard, *Oeuvres choisies de Tertullien et de saint
Augustine* (1845), 24.

we can read in the *Corpus Hermeticum* this invective against the dualist sects: they are called 'Sons of Typhon'.[45]

What remains to consider are two extreme examples characteristic of a quite distinct original corruption:

- The first, of an orgiastic type, is "by no means…a question of a false *morality,* the result of a culpable abandon to the deviated instincts of our nature, but of a *spiritual* and metaphysical fault, by which one intends to prove to oneself and to others that one is truly free of all duality and every distinction, even of that distinction between sacrilege and the sacred."[46]
- The second, of a satanic type, exemplifies, according to Guénon, "the counterinitiation, in other words of all that which, in revolt against the divine order, undertakes to use the power inherent in sacred forms contrary to their true sense."

Both finally represent "an inverted parody that takes the infranatural for the supernatural."[47] Obviously, these perversions, wrongly referred to as gnostic, are inherently anti-gnostic. That is why, when we reread the texts of Irenaeus and Clement, it is clear that the Christian heresiologists stand against the sacrilegious claim of those who define themselves as 'gnostic' without necessarily implying a particular categorization.[48]

The truly-named Gnosis

Expertise in any field has its limits — and the literature on this subject is immense! But, nothing seems to prove that "the term 'Gnostic'…has an identifiable heresiological value."[49] How, indeed, could it be otherwise when the term 'gnosis' is accepted in some way by the primitive tradition of Christianity? Why would heresiologists always want to denounce the heretics' abuse

---

45 Jean Doresse, "L'hermétisme égyptianisant," *Histoire des religions*, tome II (Paris: Pléiade), 474.

46 *The Secret of the Christian Way,* 15.

47 Ibid., 16.

48 Ibid., 10.

49 Ibid.

of *gnosis* and agree without further concern when the enemies of the Church called themselves 'gnostics'?

St. Paul is first to reveal the lie of 'pseudo-gnosis' (1 Tim. 6:20) — *anthitheseis tes pseudonymou gnoseos* ("the contradictions of the falsely named gnosis") — defending the very word *gnosis*. Why does he speak of a 'falsely named' and not just of a true or false knowledge? "His formula can only mean one thing: true knowledge is also *the* knowledge par excellence, that unique knowledge which, for this reason alone, must have reserved for it the term *gnosis*."[50] That is why St. Paul can say elsewhere (1 Cor. 8:1–7) that "We all have gnosis" and "not everyone has the gnosis," since gnosis can be either a simple theoretical knowledge which as such is an 'ignorant' knowledge full of itself or the effective realization of knowledge's transcendent and divine nature which protects it from any outside 'aggression': the *learned ignorance* of Nicholas of Cusa. From then on this tradition is in place:

- Thus St. Irenaeus does not denounce gnosis in his *Adversus Haereses*, but rather 'the gnosis with a false name' as the original title (preserved for us by Eusebius of Caesarea and St. John of Damascus) suggests: *Elenkos kai anatrope tes pseudonymou gnoseos*.[51]
- St. Clement of Alexandria, the pre-eminent doctor of Christian gnosis, does not say otherwise when defining the gnostic as the perfect Christian, the one who has achieved the perfect knowledge of Christ. In other words, the term 'gnostic' does not imply that the subject belongs to a sect or religious school, but that he has attained a *spiritual state*.[52]
- Origen also refers to this 'gnosis of God' that few men possess and by which Moses entered the divine darkness.[53]
- From St. Evagrius of Pontus to St. Simeon the New Theologian, the spiritual theology of Greek Christianity has inherited the tradition of this term.[54]

---

50 Ibid.
51 *Problèmes de gnose*, 19.
52 *The Secret of the Christian Way*, 11.
53 *Contra Celsum*, VI, 17; *Sources chrétiennes*, n° 147, p. 220; *Problèmes de gnose*, 19.
54 *The Secret of the Christian Way*, 11.

The fact that St. Paul is almost the only New Testament writer to speak of gnosis is certainly evidence of the influence of the Septuagint Bible, the first to give to this term an essentially religious connotation. Thus, compared to St. John the Evangelist, who is the most gnostic of the New Testament writers,[55] Paul, that great man of rabbinic science, is more focused on concepts; the Evangelist, whose knowledge has its source in the direct vision of Gnosis incarnate, Jesus Christ, mainly uses major traditional symbols, such as sheep and shepherd, light and darkness, to express himself.

And this shows us a second — less circumstantial — reason why St. Paul speaks of gnosis. Among the founding authorities of Revelation as recognized by Christian dogma, St. Paul is, paradoxically, one of the 'pillars of the Church', a custodian of the authentic message, even though he never "knew Christ in the flesh."[56] He is the unique case whose word has revelatory value because, besides the teaching he undoubtedly received from the Apostles, he received the revelation of the Gospel directly from the Lord (1 Cor. 11:23). "Christian dogmatics therefore recognizes that there is at least a revelation that comes not only from the 'historic' Christ but also from the internal Son that God, says St. Paul, 'revealed within myself'" (Gal. 1:17). In other words, it admits that there may be a 'spiritual' experience worthy of revelation, a mode of knowledge by which the pneumatised intellect participates in the knowledge that God has of Himself in His Word. This experience "is willed by God as a doctrinal norm and benchmark of the Christian faith, *yet without constituting a 'second revelation'*. . . . It is to this mode of knowledge [this spiritual state] which realizes the perfection of faith that St. Paul gives the name of gnosis."[57]

---

55 St. John's writings show the highest number of repetitions of *ginôskô* and *oïda* (*eïdénaï* infinitive: 'to know'), but no noun to define knowledge. Cf. *Concordance de la Bible. Nouveau Testament* (Éd. Du Cerf and Desclée de Brouwer, 1970); *Problèmes de gnose*, 38. In addition, according to some scholars (C.H. Dodd, in particular) the Fourth Gospel was essentially written to prove that true gnosis is faith in Jesus Christ, and to attest to the saving power of "His Name" (John 20:31); cf. *Problèmes de gnose*, 20.

56 "Every Christian must believe that all of Revelation was given in Jesus Christ and the Apostles are its authorized recipients because only they have received it. . . . Compared to this direct revelation (written or oral), which alone is authoritative, there can only be private revelations (devoid of the authority of faith) or theological commentaries which explain what is revealed" (*Problèmes de gnose*, 39).

57 Ibid.

To continue with this attempt at definition, we can say that the "gnosis is ... a supernatural and unifying knowledge of Divine Reality. The three following elements are indeed essential to its definition:

1. Divine Reality or infinite and perfect Reality — because all knowledge is specified by its object and that of gnosis is none other than the object par excellence, the absolutely real;
2. Unifying or identifying knowledge — because, unlike with any other knowledge, we are in the presence of gnosis only if there is transformation of the knowing subject and union with the known Object; while knowledge, operating by abstraction, normally leaves the very being of the knower outside of itself, here this takes place precisely only with a deifying participation with what it knows;
3. Supernatural, metaphysical, supra-rational or sacred knowledge — because, while being entirely about knowledge, like any speculative act, it differs radically by its mode, which is that of the pneumatized (or spiritual) intellect; indeed, it differs from other modes to the extent that with this knowledge is realized the perfecting of all cognitive aspirations.

This vision of a sacred intellectuality is, in essence, what Plato and the Neo-Platonists sought to implement: a knowledge that is a conversion and engages the whole being in such a way that the degrees of knowledge are so many hierarchically ascending states of the being. The symbol of the Cave teaches this,[58] as well as Plotinus's doctrine of hypostases."[59]

Such a gnosis — "an immense and sacrosanct reality, a profound and mysterious reality" that early Christians referred to among themselves without feeling the need to explain further — is this interior and intimate 'science' of God, the effective and deep-seated awareness of the Spirit infusing the soul of the believer with the grace of Jesus Christ; in short, the realization of faith. That is why a poorly understood Gnosis is vainglorious, to which St. Paul would add: "Gnosis puffs up, charity edifies. If anyone imagines that he

---

58 Cf. *infra*, Chap. 5: "The Metaphysics of Analogy," especially the "Cave and Analogy" section.

59 *Problèmes de gnose*, 164–65.

knows something, he does not yet know as he ought to know" (1 Cor. 8:2–3). Thus, "true gnosis does not pose as knowledge one could speak about and be dazzled with, but is in some manner 'unknown' to itself."[60]

The writings of St. Clement describe the spiritual state of someone who has reached the end of the Christian way, and, therefore the knowledge of Christ:

- "The gnostic is consequently divine and already holy, God-bearing and God-borne";[61]
- "The Word impresses on the gnostic the seal of the perfect contemplation, according to His own image, so that there is now a third divine image";[62]
- His very body becomes spiritual;[63]
- "The gnostic has created himself,"[64] which is comparable to the Islamist aphorism *as-Sufi lam yukhlaq* ("the Sufi is not created").[65]

To complete the parallel we will quote another Muslim spiritual saying: "In the beginning Sufism was a reality without a name, today it is a name without a reality." This is ever the risk of (Christian) gnosis, its risk of decaying into gnosticism.[66]

But gnosis is not just charismatic and interior, even if this is its deepest and most decisive aspect. It is also this "strictly intellectual activity that is able to formulate and express itself clearly and accurately. From this point of view, Paul opposes glossolalia, a vague and inarticulate 'speaking in tongues,' to 'speaking in gnosis,' which uses meaningful articulations of the language to convey knowledge and doctrine, and therefore to 'build up' the community (1 Cor. 14:6–19)." Both internal and ineffable, gnosis is also able to be formulated and serve as an objective doctrinal *corpus*; and so it is transmissible

60 *The Secret of the Christian Way*, 10.

61 *Stromata*, VII, 13, 82.

62 Ibid., VII, 3, 16. The first two images are without the shadow of a doubt the Word and His humanity.

63 Ibid., VII, 14; cf. Fénelon, *Le gnostique* (Paris: Gabriel Beauchesne, 1930).

64 Ibid., VII, 13, 3. A non-pantheist understanding of this 'self-creation' is found in Jean Borella, *The Sense of the Supernatural* (Edinburgh: T & T Clark, 1998), chap. 8.

65 René Guénon, *Insights into Islamic Esoterism and Taoism* (Hillsdale, NY: Sophia Perennis, 2001), 50.

66 *The Secret of the Christian Way*, 12.

and can be the subject of a tradition. It is even essential that gnosis consists of these two aspects: thus it is "neither an abstract theory, a vain conceptuality illusorily content with its own formulations, or a confused mysticism only too eager to take refuge in the incommunicable."[67]

Doctrinal Gnosis, Faith, and Full Gnosis

"Man is essentially and first of all an intellectual being, a knowing being, even though this knowing may be of the most humble sensory kind; as loudly and keenly as desire might speak within him, it speaks to someone who hears and recognizes it, someone for whom it makes sense or is repudiated. Man is never a desiring machine. But neither is he a believing machine, a 'religious automaton' invested with some wholly external revelation or salvation completely incongruous to his nature."[68]

The reception of — supernatural — revelation in the intelligence of the believer requires that he has a natural capacity for intelligibility at his disposal. "By understanding revelation, the intellect understands itself as well . . . and if this self-understanding is not an idealistic reduction of what is revealed to the *a priori* conditions for knowledge of the human subject, it is because these intelligible forms are naturally ordered to metaphysical and supernatural realities."[69]

This is the 'gnostic moment' of the act of faith: the intellective receptivity appropriate for revelation is taught and communicated through language. It is therefore an act of knowledge that is also necessarily speculative. However, this is not a simple exercise of natural reason but "an actualization of those theomorphic possibilities implied by man's creation 'in the image of God' . . . an intrinsically sacred intellectuality [made of] those *spermatikoi logoi*, those 'figures' of the Divine Word sown in every intellect (the light of the Word 'enlightens *every* man coming into this world' [John 1:9]), and is therefore a kind of inward and congenital 'revelation' of those intellective icons — the metaphysical Ideas — immanent to the soul."[70]

This doctrinal gnosis is based on an awareness of metaphysical and theological intellectuality. As intellectuality, it is only the natural act of an intellect

---

67 *Problèmes de gnose*, 40.
68 *The Secret of the Christian Way*, 20.
69 Ibid.
70 Ibid., 21.

working according to its own requirements; as "sacred, it grasps its own contents as a grace of the Word radiating within itself." However, this doctrinal gnosis — ordered to the reception of revelation: a genuine *metaphysics of welcome* — is not the whole of gnosis; "the gnostic first fruits to the act of faith assume their full meaning only in faith itself."[71]

A scriptural basis for this doctrine and, more generally, for the order required to implement the act of faith is signified in the Prologue of St. John's Gospel precisely by the order of its recitation. First to be taught is the metaphysical science necessary for revelation to make sense to the intellect: the Divine Word is the eternal Gnosis of the Father and it is the Word that communicates to each human being his or her own capacity for cognitive enlightenment. Only then does John reveal that the Word "came to his own . . . became flesh . . . dwelt amongst us."

"When, thanks to the light of gnosis, we see the Light-made-flesh . . . the initial and initiating light is obliterated by its very transparency. The presence of the Divine Object blinds every other knowledge, and gnostic consciousness must somehow renounce itself." By renouncing itself, gnosis somehow enters the darkness of faith. What was light (of knowledge) becomes obscurity (of faith). But "only by this renunciation can its very nature be transformed . . . [be] converted into and united with its Object." This is what, from Hegel to Heidegger, "philosophism rejects, namely *the absorption of knowledge into its own transcendent contents.*"[72]

"The severed head of the Forerunner [John the Baptist] 'realizes' the truth of 'partial gnosis,' the one that St. Paul says is ours *now* (1 Cor. 13:12). . . . By losing its 'head' this Johannine gnosis enters into the mystery of infinite ignorance. Created being, that which is not-God, becomes identified with its own ontological ignorance."

"This consummation of partial gnosis, which becomes an unknowing, conditions the realization of integral gnosis. The latter, as St. Paul teaches (1 Cor. 13:13), consists in knowing as we are known. . . . This formula . . . not only postulates the analogical reciprocity of the human gnosis and Divine Gnosis, it also basically implies their essential identity. Once stripped of all particular knowledge and plunged into infinite ignorance, the intellect reaches a state of

71 Ibid., 23.
72 Ibid., 25.

perfect nakedness and pure transparency. Having thus become what it is in its depths, there is no longer anything in it to oppose its complete investment by Divine Gnosis. God knows Himself within this intellect and *as* this intellect, which is therefore only one with the Immaculate Conception that God has of Himself. This is why Mary is the sole key to this mystery of Supreme Gnosis."[73]

Modern Gnosticism

Scholars have pointed to the bias of an anti-creationist angelism (the world is bad) often evident among the so-called gnostics, and we might also mention its corollary: a christological docetism (the belief that the body of Christ was only an appearance). But what of the gnostic temptation in modern times?

First we have to contrast it with ancient gnosticism, which was always religious.

- Indeed, "if we set aside the orgiastic and 'Typhonian' countergnosis, for which there is very little documentation, the main body of ['gnostic'] writings speak only of the most lofty metaphysical, mystical and symbolic questions in the language of religion."[74] This involves one's being united with God through an awareness purified of any bodily element (its character of 'interiority') and, in its very being, an escape from the corporeal world (its 'saving' character). The two features of this knowledge — internal and saving — make of it a 'gnosis'.

- To the contrary, neo-gnosticism offers "doctrines that consider science the true religion, not in the manner of the nineteenth-century scientism, for which science must *eliminate* religion"; neo-gnosticism would rather have science "replace religion by assuming all its functions. . . . The purest type of this modern gnosticism, as found in Ruyer, obviously implies a transformation of scientific knowledge." Scientific knowledge "can only be a gnosis if it ceases to be subject to the rationalist dualism of subject (spiritual) and object (material) to become the participative knowledge of a *universe–man* continuum, a continuum indwelt under various forms by a Spirit merged with

73 Ibid., 27.
74 Ibid., 18.

Nature. Matter is spirit upside-down and inside-out. Neo-gnosticism
is the 'revelation' of this reversal that effects a kind of speculative or
theoretical 'salvation' by putting things back in place."

If neither of these two types of gnosis is the truly named gnosis it is for
opposite reasons: the first, on behalf of the divine transcendence, denies God's
immanence in the world (anti-creationism, Docetism). The second, on behalf
of immanence and even a pantheistic identification of Spirit and matter (as
with Jean E. Charon, for example), rejects all transcendence. It also rejects
any 'historical' intervention of Transcendence in the world of men. The first
one is a misunderstanding of the sacrificial Incarnation. The second is a misunderstanding of the Easter Resurrection, "where the *glorious* and spiritual
nature of the flesh itself appears" in a world indwelt by the Spirit surely, but
less perfect, less real than the Spirit.[75]

Next, it is clearly necessary to set the modern gnosticist temptation, the
so-called neo-gnosticism, back in its rightful place with a brief history of Western thought. Doing so, we will attempt to understand the 'epistemological
habits'[76] of the modern world. We have seen that gnosis corresponded to
that sacred intellectuality in which knowledge is a conversion that involves
the whole being: the degrees of knowledge being so many hierarchically
ascending states of the being. But this doctrine, Platonic in origin, will soon
encounter Aristotelian science: a single science, whatever its purpose, that
reduces all knowledge to the known reality of a single mode of abstraction
(cf. *Metaphysics*, IV, c. 2, 1004a5).

- "For Plato, to know is to know what is. The truth of knowledge can
  vary, depending on the reality of its object. Therefore, the degrees of
  knowledge strictly correspond to the degrees of reality, in such a way
  that any lower degree is ignorance compared to a higher degree. . . .
  Only Absolute knowledge (the Unconditioned, *Anhypotheton*) is
  absolutely knowledge, knowledge of the Supreme Good, 'beyond
  being' (*epekeina tes ousias* [*Republic*, VI, 509b]). But this requires an
  actualizing of the intellect (*nous*) and an abandoning of discursive

75 *Problèmes de gnose*, 25–26.
76 Cf. "Intelligence spirituelle et surnaturel," op. cit., 58.

knowledge (*dianoia*). In other words, because all true knowledge is a desire for being, the intellect cannot (really) know anything it cannot identify with. But can man become a stone, tree or cat? No. Consequently there is no perfect knowledge of the stone, tree or cat (as sensible and physical beings)."[77]

- Aristotle, who especially sought scientific certainty in the physical realm, inaugurated "what might be called 'profane science', that is, an exclusively abstract operation of knowledge." But keep in mind that his famous formula "the soul is all it knows" (*De anima*) always includes the adverb *pos* (πῶς): 'somehow' (*quodammodo*).[78] "And if the soul in the act of knowing can be *quodammodo* all things (stone, tree, cat), this is precisely because the act of knowing extracts the intelligible form from the known being. In other words, this is because, *entitatively*, the soul is nothing of what it knows, because it can be *intentionally* identified with everything known. Knowledge, for Aristotle, is achieved by a process of abstraction that 'de-existentiates' the intelligible form. It is torn away from real and concrete being and allowed to exist in the soul with which it unites by 'informing' it. The Intelligible form is then nothing more than what is called a concept." Unfortunately, what is valid for the sensible world is not so for the intelligible world (the existence of which Aristotle denies).

In any case it is Aristotle's philosophy that provides the general concept of what a science should be and, at the same time, the model of all (profane) knowledge: "to know is to know an object, that is, something which is, in its being, radically distinct from the being of the knowing subject";[79] this ontological distinction ensures the objectivity of science.

This concept is amazingly attuned to Christianity, at the time of Christianity's eruption into the cultural field of antiquity. Just as salvation is realized by faith in Christ who gives us His grace — raising human nature to its deified perfection — so simple intellective knowledge is seen to be divested of its salvific dimension. Therefore, knowledge is related to intelligence, and being to

---

77 *Problèmes de gnose*, 165–66.

78 For instance, in *De anima* III, 8, 431 b 21: *e psyche ta onta pos esti panta* ("the soul is, *in a certain way*, all beings"); our emphasis!

79 *Problèmes de gnose*, 166–67.

religion. "Hence the timeliness of a doctrine that ontologically 'neutralizes' and 'secularizes' knowledge and that leaves human existence to religion. Doing so, by sharing their respective expertise, science and faith, philosophy and religion, nature and the supernatural, reason and grace are reconciled."[80]

This equilibrium that flourished in the work of St. Thomas Aquinas is fragile:

- Faith in its very essence is knowledge, while knowledge includes a dimension of faith as an adherence of the being to what it does not yet see. This shows "in science as in faith, the *presence* of a common, irreducible *kernel of gnosis*" and amounts to a denial of any real distinction between science and faith.
- Contradictorily, their methodical distinction is radicalized so that "science is gradually defined as a non-faith, and faith, as a non-science."

Non-science-faith will be actualized by the Lutheran protest, with faith conceived of as purely fiduciary. Non-faith-science will be first actualized by Cartesianism, which will definitively marginalize theology, and then by Kantian criticism, which will reject *a priori* the ontological dimension of knowledge: the real is, by definition, what cannot be known. "The theological repercussions of Kantism, despite or because of Hegel's 'pseudo-gnostic' reaction, leads to the Bultmannian approach and the so-called death of God theologies: every concept is an alienating abstraction, even that of God . . . , faith is simply a real-life experience having no other purpose than to provoke in human life an awareness of its irremediable contingency."

This is the current intellectual situation of the Christian West, where, for philosophy, there is no knowledge that does not posit its object as a distinct reality, and, "for theology, to unite being with knowing, or to speak of a salvation for knowledge is to make void revelation and grace . . . and unfailingly fall into pantheism."[81]

Finally, we must at least mention Ruyerian and Hegelian 'gnosis' — gnosis only so-called, because in fact, the speculative vision of Ruyerian

80 "*Gnose et gnosticisme chez René Guénon,*" 115.
81 Ibid., 113–16.

cosmologism,[82] like that of Hegelian idealism, is by nature not simply scientific or philosophical (in the Kantian sense of reflexive and abstract). Indeed, such 'gnosticism' challenges the very idea of revelation — whether, as Ruyer does, by excluding any reference to Christ, or, as Hegel does, by claiming to exceed it with philosophy — but "far from separating science and religion, reason and revelation, intelligence and faith, the Hegelian and Ruyerian approaches . . . intend to open the field of a 'scientific' knowledge which is, by itself, also an almost mystical participation in the being of things."[83] Thus, Hegel can say that "the esoteric thinking about God and identity, like that about knowledge and concepts, is philosophy itself."[84] "Similarly, with Ruyer (who wrote at least two books on God), the ambition to be the 'theologian' of modern science is undeniable. The theme of ontological participation (to be is to participate in a God-Universe) underlies all his thinking."[85] If we reject Hegelian 'gnosis' (as immanent panlogism) as well as Ruyerian 'gnosis' (since it is cut off from its proper spiritual and supernatural dimension), it does not "seem possible however to reject the *need for gnosis* as such, seeing that the root of every intellective aspiration is recognized therein. For it is just this that is at work here. In their excesses, limitations, or even deviations, Hegelianism, like Ruyerism or Spinozism, betrays a demand native to the human intellect that is the sense and expectation of true being, the sense of the absolutely real within us. This is an unassailable fact. Man is, in essence, primarily an intellectual being, primarily a being of knowledge."[86]

As for the other modern 'gnosticisms' — paradoxically lacking in this same *gnostic need* — they hardly seem anything but a sectarian phenomenon. "The answer to the proliferation of sects can be summarized in two strokes: restore the liturgical order and the beauty of its *mystery*; reopen in the understanding of faith the door to gnosis."[87]

82 Raymond Ruyer, *La gnose de Princeton* (Paris: Arthème Fayard, 1974), 17 n.1 and 264–92.

83 *Problèmes de gnose*, 61.

84 *Encyclopédie des sciences philosophiques en abrégé*, trans. Gandillac (Paris: Gallimard, 1970), 499.

85 *La gnose de Princeton*, 70–71, 73 and above all 130 : "Gnosis consists in wanting to have the participables enter into science as into religious philosophy, through the front door...in order to show that science reveals participation, but only by seeing it inside out."

86 *Secret of the Christian Way*, 19–20.

87 "Intelligence spirituelle et surnaturel," op. cit., 59.

THREE

The Four Modes of Theology

In his 2002 work Lumières de la théologie mystique (Insights into Mystical
Theology) *— that is, mystical theology as distinguished from a theology of mysticism —Jean Borella has collected the most helpful guidance for understanding
theology—inseparable from Christianity—as a spiritual and initiating way
rather than mere speculation or an intellectual exercise—even if we see that,
according to the Dionysian doctrine, these approaches are far from being unconnected, insofar as the intellect proves to be 'naturally supernatural'.*[1]

*To be complete, our presentation should include, besides issues of compatibility
between theology and intelligence and theology and reason, many distinctions
covering the entire history of theology: its form and object, the three philosophical
conceptions of theology, the three axes of theology in early Christianity, and the
three sources of theological science and the four ways of theology according to
St. Dionysius the Areopagite.*

*Only the latter two topics will be presented here. The first article, 'The three
sources of theological science', ushers us into the Dionysian theological tradition.
The second, 'The four ways of theology', gives us a taste of this ascensional theology
that culminates, beyond every height, in mystical theology.*

*Of course, the summary of the 'theory of practical theology' presented here
will be missing all the illustrations compiled by Jean Borella and, one might
even say, the very contents of this initiatory theology, especially the renowned
and sublime texts of St. Dionysius the Areopagite, Meister Eckhart, the blessed
Henry Suso and the unknown author of the* Theologia Germanica, *texts to be
found in Jean Borella's* Lumières de la théologie mystique.

---

1 *Amour et vérité,* 116.

The Three Sources of Theological Science

According to Dionysius, the grace of theological knowledge can be received in three ways: Scripture, oral Tradition, and interior illumination. The third way, having the first two as prerequisites and distinct from tradition, is 'theoretical knowledge' or *mathon* (from *mathein*: knowledge), inasmuch as *pathon* (from *pathein*: experience): 'living experience'.[2] Those three sources correspond to the three modes of theological gnosis:

- 'Theopathic' intellection is the subjective mode,
- Scripture is the objective mode,
- And tradition comes from both of these: the transmission of the objective deposit between living subjects.

Sources of the grace of theological knowledge		Modes of theological gnosis	
ILLUMINATION	*Pathon*	Subjective	'lived experienced'
TRADITION	*Mathon*	Mixed	'theoretical knowledge'
SCRIPTURE		Objective	

This Illumination is not at all illuministic. It cannot be dissociated from prayer or, in particular, from the sacraments. It is a 'divine initiation', an "intellectual light that inwardly assimilates us to its Divine Object." It is a "kind of sacrament . . . because it only occurs under the effect of the sacrament, which is itself an 'illumination.'" Even if "our intelligence *naturally* has the power to receive enlightenment, it still has to receive it"; there is "no theognosic initiation without initiation to baptism, confirmation and the Eucharist." "The intellect's ability to be naturally ordered to the supernatural is only actualized by the sacramental initiation to divine sonship."[3] Only then are we "partakers of the divine nature" (St. Peter) or "ontologically grafted onto God by baptism" (Jean Borella), and from that moment on "subsist divinely" (Dionysius).

---

2 According to the pun by Aristotle related by Synesius of Cyrene. Cf. N. Turchi, *Fontes Historiae Mysteriorum Aevi Hellenistici*, no. 83 (Rome, 1930), 53; *Lumières de la théologie mystique*, 85.

3 *Lumières de la théologie mystique*, 86.

The basic principle of Scripture is that, according to Denys in particular, it contains all possible knowledge of God: "We must avoid applying any word or any thought recklessly to the superessential and secret Deity with the exception of what has been divinely revealed to us by the Scriptures."[4] Of course, this is not "the limit of all theology: it is only the limit of the sayable."[5]

As for tradition, it should first be noted that Scripture is first transmitted by tradition. Tradition, moreover, is Scripture's 'living continuity', with "the key to the intelligibility of the divine Word."[6] This living and understandable transmission is, along with the administration of the sacraments, the major function of the ecclesiastical institution. Whether scripturial tradition is written or oral — in the latter case, it may also be secret (*kruphia parado-sis*) — the sacramental tradition may be called symbolic (*symbolike paradosis*): "This initiation that we can refer to as symbolic of the holy birth of God in us [baptism] . . . contains . . . no sensible image, but reflects the enigmas of a contemplation worthy of God in natural mirrors adapted to human faculties."[7]

THEOLOGY				
ILLUMINATION	Prayer			
	Initiatic sacrament			
TRADITION	Administration of sacraments	Symbolic	Major role of the ecclesial institution	
	Transmission Of the Word	Written		
		Oral	Secret	
SCRIPTURE	All possible knowledge of God			

The Four Ways of Theology

This Dionysian context has clarified the conditions of a theology which is much more initiation than speculation. Now we have to introduce the four modes or ways that can lead, by grace, to the *knowledge* of God.

4 Dionysius the Areopagite, *Divine Names*, 585 B, 67; *Lumières de la théologie mystique*, 87.
5 *Lumières de la théologie mystique*, 87.
6 Ibid., 88.
7 Dionysius the Areopagite, *Ecclesiastical Hierarchy*, 397 A–B, 256; *Lumières de la théologie mystique*, 89.

Starting from the Scriptures — which is the rule — we see that they speak of God through images (the Rock, the Light) or through concepts (the Good, Being, Life). The images correspond to *symbolic theology,* while the concepts relate to *cataphatic* (affirmative) *theology.* Divine transcendence on the other hand requires that any assertion about God be denied: this is *apophatic* (negative) *theology.* Finally, even beyond any denial (saying what God is not), apophatic theology ends in the non-modal mode of *mystical theology,* "the 'place' of What is placeless." These four ways or modes appear as "four stages of a single ascent of knowledge,"[8] for which, as we shall see, Love is the elevating agent.

MYSTICAL THEOLOGY		Non Modal	
APOPHATIC THEOLOGY		Negative	
CATAPHATIC THEOLOGY		Affirmative	Notions (Good, One, Life...)
SYMBOLIC THEOLOGY		Symbolic	Images (Rock, Light...)
	Love		

Symbolic Theology

Symbolic theology consists in making explicit the theological nature of symbols. Essentially cosmological (by nature), symbols drawn from Scripture are offered to our intelligence for it to "read in these forms an instruction that escapes any form,"[9] so to grasp "featureless realities in the features of these realities":[10] the Rock and the Light symbolize (or make present) God.

If the symbol is a link between visible and invisible, this is because it is a 'dissimilar similarity',[11] and this contradiction is intrinsic to the nature of the symbolic link:

- The similarity that links, statically, the visible to the invisible, is the *analogic* nature of symbol.
- The dissimilarity that leads to the renouncing of the image and, *dynamically,* raises up the image towards its model is its anagogical virtue (the anagogical act being literally 'a raising up').

8 *Lumières de la théologie mystique,* 94.
9 René Roques, Introduction à la *Hiérarchie céleste* (Paris: Sources Chrétiennes, 1958), 58, p. xxi; *Lumières de la théologie mystique,* 95.
10 *Lumières de la théologie mystique,* 95.
11 René Roques, *L'univers dionysien,* 201, n. 2; *Lumières de la théologie mystique,* 103.

SYMBOL		Unfigured Reality			
	NATURE OF THE SYMBOLIC LINK			SYMBOLIC VIRTUE	
	Dissimilarity			**Anagogic**	Dynamic
	Similarity			**Analogic**	Static
		Figured reality			

Theology being a way to God, it is normal to find in it a trend of thought that is, in this case, vertical, straight and upward.

Affirmative Theology

With *affirmative theology*, we enter the field of discursive reason's intelligible concepts, and thus of a language necessary for understanding concepts or ideas about God. As these are found initially in Scripture and transmitted by Tradition, this *notional* theology is wholly legitimate. Therefore, it is the duty of the theologian[12] to comment upon and explain all these notions issuing from Scripture: Life, Cause, Principle, etc.

In addition, this theology's discourse should be carried out from top to bottom, so that any successive statements are initially established as close to God as possible. This descending order is in imitation of the *proodos*, the procession of the divine immanence according to the degree of Creation: One or Good, Being, Life, Intelligence. . . . This descent that, on one hand, secures affirmative theology as closely to God as possible tends to be, on the other, "less and less true and somehow exhausts its own possibility."[13]

But this 'descent' is only methodological and is unrelated to the *movement of the soul* which accompanies this affirmative theology, both helping to distinguish it from symbolic theology and introducing negative theology as a necessary complement:

- As already mentioned, the movement of the soul is upward and *longitudinal* when, seeing God in nature, it rises from effect to cause, from the figure to the Model (symbolic theology);
- it is *helical* when the soul moves according to discursive reason (affirmative theology);

12 *Lumières de la théologie mystique*, 102.
13 Ibid., 98.

- it is *circular* when the soul "detaches itself from the multiplicity of external objects" and, with concentration, unifies "its intellective powers" (negative theology). This movement is the only one appropriate to any 'intelligible union'[14] (mystical theology).

Notice here the intermediary role of affirmative theology, illustrated by a helical motion that combines straight and circular movements.[15] Also, if this motion is the result of the discursive intelligence (*diexodikos* is the Dionysian term), to negative theology will correspond the intuitive intelligence (*noeros*).[16] Finally, if words are to be used to illustrate the fundamental contribution of each of these three theologies (i.e., symbolic, affirmative and negative), it seems that the three concepts of vision, (rational) speech, and (intellectual) intuition are appropriate.

THEOLOGY	FEATURES			MOVEMENT OF THE SOUL
MYSTICAL				
NEGATIVE	Inner concentration	Intuitive intelligence *noeros*	Intuition	*Circular*
AFFIRMATIVE	Reasoning	Discursive intelligence *diexodikos*	Speech	*Helical*
SYMBOLIC	External contemplation		Vision	*Longitudinal*

Negative Theology

Negative theology consists in "denying any symbol and any notion applied to What is beyond every figure and every name."[17] In addition, far beyond a simple denial that would contradict anything previously asserted about God, negative theology emerges as an anagogy of affirmative theology. The denied concept simply stops indicating a mental object to become "the sign of an

---

14 Dionysius the Areopagite, *Divine Names*, 705 A–B, 102–3; *Lumières de la théologie mystique*, 98.

15 *Lumières de la théologie mystique*, 99, n. 215.

16 Ibid., 110.

17 Ibid., 99.

operation performed by the theological intelligence"; conceptual language is transformed into a metaphysical operator!

Indeed, just as the symbol by its anagogic virtue allows the image not to be taken for reality, so the word (or the notion it designates, or the concept by which the notion is thought) acquires its true value when our mind becomes aware of the inadequacy of the concept to its object, when the anagogic intelligence ceases to be considered a mental thing but becomes aware of the transcendent reality it designates.

Thus, the theological intelligence perceives "the model as transcendent to its reflection in thought."[18] What might be termed 'anagogic tension'[19] is the awareness of this "tension that holds sway between the intellective essence of a notion and the mental mode of its existence, between the transcendent content of what is thought and the act (the concept) that thinks it."[20]

In other words, negative theology can help "achieve the unity of seeing (symbol) and conceiving (notion), of the symbol (vision without intellection) and the concept (intellection without vision) in the intellective vision."[21] This intellective vision, that is a 'gnosis by unknowing' having renounced any conceptual knowledge, relates then to mystical theology.

Mystical Theology

From here on *mystical theology* is only distinguished from negative theology by being the end of the path of the path itself. Once the former has denied every symbol and concept, the latter can make its appearance. When intelligence does not see the concept as a mental thing, because it denied it, because *it has closed its eyes,* then it can become aware of informal and anonymous Reality. Then it has the "decisive and paradoxical experience of its own limitations and suddenly experiences itself as a pure capacity for contemplative worship."[22]

18 Ibid., III.
19 Ibid., 101, 107, III. See also Jean Borella, *The Crisis of Religious Symbolism*, 368–9.
20 *Lumières de la théologie mystique*, III.
21 Ibid., 99.
22 Ibid., 10–II.

THEOLOGY			
MYSTICAL	Intellective Essence	Gnosis by unknowing (Intellective vision)	Transcendent content of thought
NEGATIVE	Methodological negation	Realization of the unity of seeing and conceiving	Anagogic tension
AFFIRMATIVE	Concepts	Intellection without vision	Act of thinking
SYMBOLIC	Symbols	Vision without intellection	

Obviously such an accomplishment stems at once from both knowledge and love. But what love and what knowledge are we talking about?

- Basically, the "anagogic power is the work of Love and conveys the operation of the Holy Spirit to the heart of the intellect."[23] "Love is the very movement of *theologia*, the dynamic power that makes it…pass beyond names and forms. And this erotic power in the created intellect is nothing but its *participation* in the divine *Eros* itself, in the Spirit of Love that is God in his Trinitarian ecstasy."[24]
- The Knowledge we refer to is also by *participation*. In saying 'God' and yet denying Him as a concept, what remains is the intellectual intuition — which "is the very life of the spirit" — the intelligence seized by a meaning to the very extent that the intellect becomes one with the intelligible. The metaphysical objectivity in which is unified knower, known and knowledge is intrinsic and qualitative, while "physical objectivity is extrinsic and relative: it is only the reflection of the latter which establishes it ontologically."[25] We have then surpassed every noetic operation (the order of knowledge which implies, even in the case of intellectual intuition, some speculative activity[26]) for an *ontonoesis* where being and knowing are inseparably unified.

If the anagogic power is the work of the Spirit in the intellect, this is possible because it finds, "in the intellect itself, a supra-conceptual capacity that awakens and actualizes the apophatic task: grace presupposes the nature that it perfects."[27] And so the deepest nature of our intelligence is pure intuition: not as an intellective act, but as a *supernatural nature*, a virtual identity between the intellect itself and the meaning by which the intellect is seized. By exceeding the noetic, "it is obeying not only the attraction of divine Love, but also its own internal necessity." This is why the circular movement of the soul symbolizes the *conversion of intelligence to itself*.[28] And this conversion is a continual necessity.

Negative and mystical theologies thus prove to be "a 'Passover' of the intellect,"[29] a spiritual path comprised of death and resurrection: "Death to affirmative concepts . . . that become signs of their own surpassing; resurrection, because the intellect that has consented . . . to its own obliteration, its own crucifixion, is established in a supereminent state of 'gnosis by unknowing.'" These two extinctive and unitive moments are revealed precisely by the death and resurrection of Christ. "The stripping away of all intellectual operations, the renouncing of every particular object in order to recognize the divine Object alone, this is the putting to death of an intelligence crucified with Christ. And this intelligence, like Him, having renounced any intelligible form of the divine, can only cry out: *Eli, Eli, lamma sabacthani*. . . . Baptized into the death of Christ, the paschal intellect is resurrected with Him."[30]

Because in Christianity, "there can be no other way of gnosis than Jesus Christ Himself, the incarnation of the *Logos*, that is to say the knowledge that God has of Himself. . . . And this is why from Origen to Meister Eckhart, and for the greatest mystics, the knowledge of God, true gnosis, is identical to divine sonship: Knowing God means becoming 'Sons.'"[31]

APPENDIX: TWO ILLUSTRATIONS OF SYMBOLIC THEOLOGY

Before presenting these illustrations, that is, the semeion *of St. John the Evangelist and the icon of Rublev, it may be useful to recall to what extent a symbol is a specific species of the genus sign, and how, initially combining nature and culture (e.g., water and its signification of purity), these elements are fused into a unique and irreducible entity, a fundamental metaphysical tool that breaks open*

27 Ibid., 110.
28 Ibid.
29 Ibid., 108.
30 Ibid., 108–9 & 115–16.
31 Ibid., 43.

the linguistic reduction of 'signified and signifier', and reveals a transcendent Causality. And so, to begin, a brief consideration of the symbolic sign is needed to serve as a grounding for a deeper appreciation of these 'living symbols' that are the words and Word of scripture and iconic art.

THE ANALYTICS OF THE SYMBOLIC SIGN

To speak of symbolic signs means that the symbol can be ranked under the category of sign, which is also the genus of which the symbol is a particular species. For if sign can be opposed to symbol, this is in the same Aristotelian fashion in which man is a reasonable animal. Actually, insofar as he is a living being, man is a mammal, although from another point of view he surpasses all animality and therefore transcends this category. And so for the symbol: if the natural vantage point for man is the animal kingdom, the natural vantage point for the symbol is the semiotic field, even though it itself transcends this field.

Species of Sign

That a structure is unintelligible apart from a function is illustrated by the example of two crosses — one on a roadway sign and one a sacred ornament — which would be morphologically indistinguishable, but nonetheless would constitute two basically distinct semiotic entities. What follows from this is that, first, "what defines the category of sign is not the semiotic entities that it includes, but only the signifying function"; and, second, "what defines the particular species of the semiotic genus are the various modes according to which the semiotic function is exercised." What variations may the signifying function admit of, then? Since the signifying function establishes a relationship between a signifier (or semiotic entity) and a thing signified (*signatum*, *res significativa*, referent or thing denoted) and since it is not insofar as it relates the signifier to the referent that it can vary, it must therefore be in the manner in which it effects this relationship that it can do so. Hence, what will make the modes of signification vary is the basis (or the reason) itself of the relationship of signification. This basis corresponds to the 'why', whereas the mode corresponds to the 'how', even if it might happen that these two are only one. And the three possible bases for the act by which a signifier designates a referent are causal power, traditional institution and ontological correspondence.

This is what an analysis of the different types of signs, especially those presented in scholastic treatises,[32] will make more precise. These treatises indicate two types of signs and their combination:

- Natural signs, such as tears being related to sadness or smoke to fire (or *signa naturalia* for St. Augustine)
- Institutional signs (or arbitrary signs, *ad placitum* or *signa data* — given signs — for St. Augustine), when the signifier is connected to the referent by virtue "of a choice of men or of God"
- Mixed signs, such as sacramental signs (baptismal water, for example) — and therefore symbols — which come about from a convention, but are founded on the nature of things:[33] "From their very nature sensible things have a certain aptitude for the signifying of spiritual effects: but this aptitude is fixed by the Divine institution to some special signification."[34]

Now this summary classification does not avoid confusions; in particular, it situates symbols in a hybrid category where the natural portion would be grouped together, both smoke, the sign of fire, and water, the sign of purification! Considering the examples of natural signs offered by St. Augustine — smoke, the sign of fire; an animal's tracks, the sign of its passage; the cries of a child, the sign of what it wants — we recognize rather what the Stoics call *semeion* (to be distinguished from *semainon*: linguistic sign) and what Father D. Dubarle translates quite rightly by 'epistemic sign', because this kind of sign characteristically results from the growth of our knowledge (there is a fire, an animal has passed through here . . .) or what medicine once called semiology (symptomology today). Here, the ground for the signifying relation is clearly and basically causality in the broad sense (fire causes smoke, an animal leaves

32 For example, *Philosophia scholastica*, by D. Barbedette, tome I, 26–27; *Histoire et théorie du symbole*, 202.

33 *D.T.C.*, article *signe*, tome XIV, col. 2054; *Histoire et théorie du symbole*, 202.

34 St. Thomas Aquinas (*Summa Theologiae* III, q. 64, a. 2) summarizing the doctrine formulated by St. Augustine (*De doctrina christiana*, I. II, n. 3); *Histoire et théorie du symbole*, 203, note 6.

tracks . . .) and an overly imprecise notion of a natural sign: smoke is the sign of fire only in the unusual circumstance that the fire is invisible or is a miracle attributed to God in a rather supernatural fashion. This sign-effect that leads to the need for a cause might be called an inductive sign. This inductive sign corresponds to the fourfold pattern of the sign, as the example of smoke, the sign of fire, illustrates:

- the signifier is the smoke,
- the objective referent is the fire,
- the meaning that enables us to pass from one to the other is the idea, known by experience, that fire is the cause of smoke,
- the intelligible referent is the general notion of causality viewed in its metaphysical reality.

Here we recognize, according to the teaching of Raymond Ruyer, that the notion of causality "surpasses by far that of a simple determinism with which it is too often identified, since it implies the unity of a cosmic, transpatial and transtemporal 'theme' or 'idea,' of which physical determinism is, by degrees, the only observable trace, and which, in its principial and metacosmic root, is nothing but the creative power of *natura naturans*."[35]

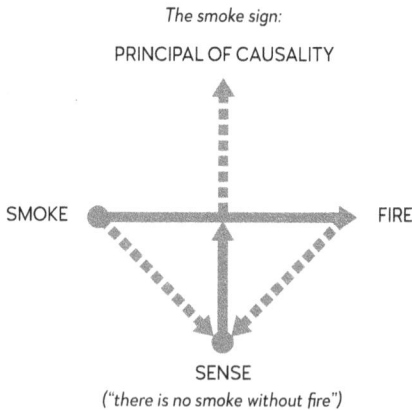

The smoke sign:

PRINCIPAL OF CAUSALITY

SMOKE ●━━━━━━━━➤ FIRE

SENSE
("there is no smoke without fire")

---

35 Jules Lachelier, in his work *Du fondement de l'induction* (Alcan, 1916, 7th ed., 97–102), presents a quite similar thesis; cf. *Histoire et théorie du symbole*, 206, note 14.

As for the institutional, here are some necessary remarks which will introduce us to the symbolic sign:

- As pointed out, this species of sign ignores the distinction of mode and basis, at least formally. In fact, a pure convention "is the idea of a relationship that is its own basis for itself: 'this is so because we have decided upon it'"; this species of sign is foreign to the nature of the terms that it brings into relation so that, save for knowing it, it is impossible to determine the referent by a simple examination of the signifier. Thus, "the signifying function acquires a kind of autonomy, a kind of existence for itself…, [and] is no longer buried beneath the naturality of the signifier[;] it is presented and manifested in its irreducible actuality." Ultimately, the institutional sign alone truly exercises a signifying function, whereas the inductive sign is basically only an *upside-down* causal relation.
- What remains is that there is no pure convention. "To the extent that it is the work of someone, of a primordial law-giver, an Adam-logothete or God, that is, of a being who would not act without sufficient reason (his freedom rules out the arbitrary), a semantic convention necessarily shares in a certain naturality."[36]

The Symbolic Sign: the Transforming Unity of Inductive Sign and Institutional Sign

Then there is a third species of sign: the symbol. Even though, formally, it seems to combine the two previous species, being only an assemblage would take away all of its own reality, and there would no longer be any symbol as such. This is because, in the symbol, the original synthesis of the inductive and institutional — or of nature and culture — the components "undergo a complete transformation which makes them well suited for being fused into a unique and irreducible entity, however contradictory they were previously."[37] Here are then two examples where this dual transformation is evidently produced:

36 This doctrine is in conformity with that of St. Thomas Aquinas; cf. Roguet, *Les sacrements* (Paris: Le Cerf, 1952), 296; *Histoire et théorie du symbole*, 200–7.

37 *Histoire et théorie du symbole*, 208.

• The *Semeion* of St. John

The inductive sign, although it surely indicates the cause — as smoke does a fire — in fact only refers to the power of the cause, for it does not pass through to the knowledge of the cause itself. This is the case for the sign-miracle that reveals the power of God but not His Essence. Induction takes place through the mode of the sign, but the inductive sign does not lead to true knowledge: the intellectual grasp of a cause's essence. Now this is what the symbolic sign achieves: not only does it not exclude that the signifier can be the effect of a cause but, above all, "it affirms that the effect is in the image of its cause," that the cause "manifests its own essence in the effect itself, not by virtue of its causal power, but by its exemplarity, that is, the participation of the effect in the essence (or form) of the cause."

"In other words, according to the perspective of the symbolic sign, the effect is not *essentially* distinct from the cause; it is so only existentially." This means that there is no sign which is purely and exclusively inductive, but it is our manner of considering it, our intellectual gaze, which makes of it an at-times inductive, at-times symbolic sign, and at this latter time a sign of true knowledge and not only of existence.

To say that there is no longer any irreducible difference between inductive and symbolic signs is to pass "from an Aristotelian etiology to a Platonic one, from a causality by efficiency to a causality by participation." And it indeed seems we are witness to such a *passing* with St. John, who uses *semeion* to express this.[38] The formula *semeia kai terata*, which connect wonders to signs, translates the Hebrew *otot we-mophetim* where the singular *mophet* actually signifies a miracle but the singular *ot*, which translates *semeion*, by itself "designates that which guarantees or witnesses to a past agreement between two men or between God and man";[39] this is the definition of *symbolon*! During the same era Philo of Alexandria frequently connects *semeion* and *symbolon*; for example, on the subject of the trees of Paradise which

---

38 Cf. the analyses C.H. Dodd has devoted to symbolism in St. John in his *The Interpretation of the Fourth Gospel* (Cambridge & New York: Cambridge University Press, 1953), 133-43; cf. *Histoire et théorie du symbole*, 210, note 6.

39 *The Interpretation of the Fourth Gospel*, 141; *Histoire et théorie du symbole*, 210.

are "beautiful to look at" and "good to eat", he explains that the first
formula is "the *symbolon* of their contemplative value" and the second
"a *semeion* of their utilitarian and practical value."[40] If, with St. John,
"the faith produced by the *semeion* is equivalent . . . to a 'vision' of the
glory of Christ, and of God in Christ,"[41] this is because "metaphysics . . .
implicitly structures his Gospel."

If he speaks with insistence of the "*true* light" (1:9) — and *true* signifies
real here — or of the true vine or true bread (the one that comes from
heaven), this is because the visible light, vine or bread possess only the
shadow of reality: sensible realities surely, but shadows — and images —
of intelligible reality. We do not know if St. John had known Plato, but it
is certain that "in any religious philosophy [of that time] the conception
of a *kosmos noetos* in some form or other was assumed — the conception
of a world of invisible realities of which the visible world is a copy. . . .
His [St. John's] *phos alethinon* is the archetypeal light, *auto to phos*, of
which every visible light in this world[42] is a *mimema* or symbol."[43]

"Conversely, it is this participation in the eternal or heavenly archetype that establishes the reality of visible beings." Only to the extent
that the vine incarnates the eternal Idea of the Vine does "it have a
meaning and, strictly speaking, exist"![44] And the same goes for history
itself, which has consistency and reality only through whatever of the
timeless and the sacred is embodied within it. For St. John, and up
to the so-called Renaissance, to oppose historic reality to symbolic
reality, so to deny one by the other, makes no sense.

Thus, if "the inductive sign is transformed into the symbolic sign by
a conversion of the meaning of its naturality," this is because efficient
causality "is absorbed by a more profound relationship": "the ontological participation of the visible in the essence of the invisible, thanks to
which and in which it becomes the manifestation and epiphany of it."[45]

40 *Legum Allegoriae*, I, 58; cited by Dodd, op. cit., 142; *Histoire et théorie du symbole*, 211.
41 H. Urs von Balthasar, *La gloire et la croix*, tome I; *Apparition*, 112; *Histoire et théorie du symbole*, 211.
42 John designates the light of the sun in this way: *to phos tou kosmou toutou* (11:9); cf. *Histoire et théorie du symbole*, 212, note 13.
43 *The Interpretation of the Fourth Gospel*, 139–40; *Histoire et théorie du symbole*, 211–12.
44 *The Interpretation of the Fourth Gospel*, 140; *Histoire et théorie du symbole*, 212.
45 *Histoire et théorie du symbole*, 208–13.

- The Icon of Rublev

And, now, what is the transformation that the institutional sign undergoes in becoming a symbol? In Rublev's celebrated icon, known as the 'Icon of the Trinity',[46] we find a great number of elements that exist as symbols:

- Natural beings (a rock, a tree, a sky)
- Art objects (a temple, a stone table, a cup, robes, scepters)
- Persons (three seated angels)
- Geometrics forms (circle, rectangle, triangle, cross)
- Colors
- Dynamic relationships among these elements (for example, the circular movement starting with the left foot of the personage to the right…)
- Relationships of values between the colors (by contrast or rhythmic repetition)
- Proportional relationships (for example, the body of each angel is fourteen times its head while the natural proportion is seven)

The fact that these symbols signify what they signify derives from the institution, that is, from tradition or, to say it in another way, from the Christian cultural system. This is what indicates that a man provided with wings signifies an angel, the nimbi holiness, the scepters royalty, the lamb Christ and the whole of this icon the Trinity. Yes, but why do the angels, the oak, the rock, and so forth appear in a portrayal of the Trinity? This involves the representation of an Old Testament episode: the apparition of IHVH to Abraham, near the oak of Mambre, under the form of three men (or three angels) for whom Abraham prepares a meal (Gen. 18:1–15). This is then "a Christian reinterpretation of a pre-Christian event in which the Christian cultural system see the foreshadowing, the figure, the type, the symbol not of a future event,

46 See the commentaries on this 'icon of icons' in Paul Evdokimov, *The Art of the Icon: a Theology of Beauty* (Redondo Beach, CA: Oakwood Publications, 1990), 243–57, and, replicated in part from the above, in Abbé Henri Stéphane, *Introduction à l'ésotérisme chrétien* (Paris: Dervy, 1979), 164–69; the major work here remains The *Theology of the Icon* (vol. 2) by L. Oupensky (Crestwood, NY: St. Vladimir's Seminary Press, 1992); cf. *Histoire et théorie du symbole*, 214, note 18.

but of a dogmatic truth which will be revealed only later." This does not involve then secondary senses given to elements of Holy Scripture which would already possess a primary sense (such as the crossing of the Red Sea prefiguring Baptism or the sacrifice of Isaac prefiguring that of Christ), but the Christian cultural system reveals to us "what, from its own point of view, is the fundamental sense of this reality, the one that it has always had, but which could not be perceived as the Revealer, the pre-eminent Hermeneut, Christ, had not appeared as yet."

The semiotic entities have been introduced into another semantic universe, where they "enter into a vertical relationship of ontological correspondence with the realities that they symbolize." If they remain prophetic figures, it is by being '*prophecies in being*', for "from the point of view of their semantic transfiguration, the symbolic elements lose their historical situation:

- The oak of Mambre is identified with the tree of life and ultimately with the World-Axis,
- Abraham's dwelling is identified with the Church and ultimately with Mary, its heavenly prototype,
- The supper table becomes that of the Eucharistic sacrifice and ultimately suggests the sacrifice of the Lamb 'immolated from the creation of the world' (Apoc. 13:8),
- And so for the rest," the significance of each element being arranged along three hierarchically ordered planes:

DIVINE AND METACOSMIC PLANE	World-Axis	Mary	Eternal Sacrifice of the Word
CHRISTIC AND SUPERNATURAL PLANE	Tree of Life	Church	Eucharistic sacrifice
HUMAN PLANE	Oak of Mambre	Dwelling of Abraham	Supper table
EXAMPLES			

"One same nature, or essence or prototypical reality is expressed at three different levels (and at all the intermediate degrees that our three planes represent synthetically). . . . [And] this plurality of referents is not accidental to the symbol, but, to the contrary, *it is altogether essential to it*."[47]

47 *Histoire et théorie du symbole,* 213–16.

PART II

The Christian Mysterion

FOUR

Mysticism, an Integral Way

In his Christ the Original Mystery, *Jean Borella intends, as we have said, to address three issues: to indicate the limits of Guénon's definition of esotericism; to show how these limits disqualify the application of his definition of esotericism to Christianity; and to present Christianity in its own light, that is, independent of Guénonian patterns, in order to reveal its specific essence.*

The extract offered here concerns the study of the innermost sense of the Christian mysterion: *the mystical.*[1] *This sense, accepted from the fourth century to our present times, is the one where mystery — under the name of the mystical — is identified with the essence of spiritual life. However, the only significant appreciably objective sources in terms of mysticism are the sayings and writings of the mystics themselves. This excludes those inner realities or 'degrees of realization' that are unobservable and known only to God. As for Guénon, who uses mysticism as a foil for the initiatic path without giving it any specific shape (he quotes no texts and mentions only three 'mystics': Anne-Catherine Emmerich, St. John of the Cross, and Louis-Claude de Saint-Martin, the latter being very marginal from the point of view of the Catholic Church), Borella's corrections seem fundamental.*

This overview will be organized around three propositions: 1) The mystical is contemplation, 2) The mystical summons the intellect to an uplifting of itself, and 3) Theology becomes the mystical, which surpasses mysticism, morality and psychology.

---

1 The previously studied senses in *Christ the Original Mystery* are the doctrinal and sacramental senses.

The Mystical and Contemplation are paired since the Fathers of the Church

Defining, first of all, the mystical from a philological point of view, we see that it comes from *mueo* ('to initiate to the mysteries') and from which the adjective *mystikos* is derived; that is, its literal meaning is 'initiation'. With the mystery being always beyond the sayable and in invisible interiority, the 'mystical' is therefore an invitation to a journey within, a synonym for the 'esoteric'. This 'mystical' is all the more 'esoteric' when it refers to Christ ("Who has seen Me has seen the Father"), and to the One who relates all things to Christ: the Holy Spirit.

If the *mysterion* of the Scripture is Christ, secretly in the Old Testament and openly in the New, 'the mystical understanding' (*sensus mysticus*) of the 'secrets' (*arcana*) in Scripture[2] does not exhaust the Object. Moreover, this 'mystica' is already more than just doctrinal: "by receiving the evangelical Scriptures, you *see* the entire doctrine of our Savior, according to what He has said, not about the flesh that He has taken, but about his mystical body and blood" (*peri de tou mystikou somatos te kai haimatos*).[3]

Similarly, when the 'mystical' is sacramental — the Eucharist is called 'mystical liturgy'[4] or 'mystical hierurgy'[5] — it at once surpasses the plain and simple sacramental, in the sense that 'mystical symbols' (*ta mystika symbola*)[6] is distinguished from 'mystical practices' (*ta mystika éthe*).[7]

And so this adjective '*mystikos*' should not be a simple substitute for a doctrinal or sacramental sense, with an added sense of a 'spiritual experience'. Although Origen (185–c.253) founded the Christian doctrine of mystical theology, it is with St. Gregory of Nyssa (c.300–c.395) that '*mystikos*' specifically

---

2 Origen, *Homilies on Genesis and Exodus*, II, 1 (Heine trans. [Washington DC: Catholic University of America, 1982], 181); *Christ the Original Mystery*, 398.

3 Eusebius of Caesarea, *Ecclesiastical Theology*, I. 3, c. 12 ; *P.G.*, t. XXIV, col. 1021 B; *Christ the Original Mystery*, 399.

4 Eusebius of Caesarea, *Life of Constantine*, IV, 71 & 75; *P.G.*, t. XX, col. 1191 B & 1225 C; *Christ the Original Mystery*, 400.

5 Theodoret of Cyr, *Epist. 146* and *Hist. Rel.*, XIII; ed. Schultz, vol. IV, 1260 and vol. III, 1208; *Christ the Original Mystery*, 400.

6 St. Gregory of Nyssa, *Against Eunomius*, XI; *P.G.*, t. XLV, col. 860; *Christ the Original Mystery*, 400.

7 St. Gregory of Nyssa, *Against Eunomius*, XI; *P.G.*, t. XLV, col. 877 D.

comes to mean 'mystical' and the doctrine of *theoria* (contemplation) is systematically developed. *Theoria mystike* is therefore the "contemplation of the mystery in its timeless substance."[8] In this tradition, St. Macarius of Egypt (known today as Pseudo-Macarius) would originate the syntagma 'mystical union', which proved highly fruitful (*mystike synousia, unio ou unitio mystica*),[9] and which we will also find in St. Cyril of Alexandria (c.378–444).[10] This is to say that, from the late fourth century, the themes and vocabulary of Christian mysticism are in place. They will be enhanced by the Dionysian corpus of the pre-eminent mystical doctor: the enigmatic Dionysius the Areopagite and his 'Cloud of unknowing', a pure knowledge without object, a knowledge of the divine Nothing. The goal of the mystical path is unveiled at the end of the fifth (or early sixth) century.

The Mystical summons the Intellect to an Uplifting of Itself

The mystical is what is related to the Christian mystery through this mystery's triple dimension, at once sacramental, scriptural and spiritual, because "the liturgical *theoria*, the scriptural *theoria*, and the mystical *theoria* are, in the end, various aspects of one same reality."[11] In addition, if the adjective *mystikos* has replaced the noun *mysteria*, this is because a noun tells of a subject while here we must speak of an essence; to speak of it is to reveal it — *mystikos* refers more particularly to the *knowledge* of the *essence* of mysterious things.

A first level of knowledge is the simple psychological awareness of the possibility of such knowledge. At a second level, this knowledge may be called speculative if formed into a body of knowledge. But this knowledge will be mystical only if it is as secret and mysterious as those mystical realities that faith invites us to contemplate. In short, the term 'mystical' is only used by the sacred writers with the intent to summon the intellect to an uplifting of itself.

---

8 St. Gregory of Nyssa, *Hom.* 1; *P.G.*, t. XLV, col. 765; A. Daniélou, *Platonisme et théologie mystique* (Paris: Aubier, 1944), 182, n. 1; *Christ the Original Mystery*, 403.

9 St. Macarius of Egypt, *Homily 2*; *P.G.*, t. XXXIV, col. 416; D. Bouyer, *The Christian Mystery* (Edinburgh: T & T Clark, 1990), 177; *Christ the Original Mystery*, 403.

10 St. Cyril of Alexandria, *In Joannem, P.G.*, t. LXXIII, col. 161, 1045, 1048, etc.; *Christ the Original Mystery*, 403, note 4.

11 Jean Daniélou, *Platonisme et théologie mystique*, 163; *Christ the Original Mystery*, 403.

Therefore — and this is especially clear in St. Augustine (354 – 430) — "metaphysical and religious knowledge, without change of nature, is transfigured and deepened into mystical knowledge."[12] This is what the Greek Fathers call *gnosis*, which is somehow nothing other than the *life* of faith in the intellective soul. Here is clarified the paradox of a voluntary faith-adherence of intelligence to the *revelatum* and of a faith-gift of the Holy Spirit infused by baptism. Baptismal initiation communicates specifically to the intelligence in its act of adherence a *virtus gnostica,* a gnostic virtue that lifts it higher and enables it to enter into a certain connaturality with the divine mysteries.

The soul is then in "a certain nearness to the beatific vision";[13] and the 'mystical' therefore relates to contemplation, to an uplifting and finality (or perfection) of the intellect.

When Theology becomes Mystical it passes beyond Mysticism, Morality, and Psychology

Marked by the *mystical theology* of St. Dionysius, the period running from the fifth to the seventeenth century is one of a change not in the nature of contemplation, but in its vocabulary. Thus, favoring one of these two terms, John Scotus Eriugena (c.810 – c.877) still calls *theologia,* a Greek term, the highest contemplation of the divine mystery,[14] as if this *theologia* meant such a high degree of knowledge that it could not be characterized in any way.

To the contrary, in the seventeenth century, the opposite occurs: 'mystical' absorbs *theologia* and, when the latter is no longer even implied, becomes a noun and *the* mystical. From then on, having turned into a noun, the mystical, on the one hand, will lose its direct connection to the Christian *mysterion,* and on the other, will need to be properly defined and qualified (for example, as 'natural mysticism'). To this reversal of primacy between theology and mysticism will correspond the following changes in the two:

---

12 Pierre Blanchard, *Recherches augustiniennes et patristiques,* vol. II (Tribute to Father Fulbert Cayré), 1962, 311–12; *Christ the Original Mystery,* 409.

13 Dom Stolz, *Théologie de la mystique* (Chèvetogne: Ed. des Benedictins d'Amay, 1947), 190–92; *Christ the Original Mystery,* 409–10.

14 *Homily on the Prologue of John,* XIV, 16 (291 C); *Christ the Original Mystery,* 413.

- Theology loses its exclusively contemplative significance to designate only a scientifically elaborated sacred doctrine; it becomes improper as a designation for supreme gnosis.

- However, the mystical (between the tenth and thirteenth centuries) switches from a Eucharistic to an ecclesial sense. Even the *corpus mysticum* loses its Eucharistic meaning, first, because there develops a worship of the Eucharist seen and contemplated for itself as the visible Body of Christ: the *Corpus* (this is the cult of '*Jesu hostia*'); second, because of having to face heresies denying or reducing the real Eucharistic presence (such as that of Berengar of Tours in the eleventh century), the doctors are led to stress this reality by the syntagma *verum Corpus*.[15] Furthermore, the proper meaning of 'Mystical Body' is fixed as equivalent to the Church of which Christ is the head.[16]

Still considered a neologism during the late nineteenth century,[17] the term 'mysticism' made its appearance as the designation of the search for the true reality in contact with the invisible. The pejorative sense would remain, but since the second half of the twentieth century the 'mystical' has regained its right to designate that "part of theology that has as its object the supernatural relationship of the soul with God."[18]

In the meantime, a certain psychologizing of the mystical life occurred, together with a humanization of the worship of Christ (such as the cult of the Sacred Heart, which would assume some aberrant forms at the end of the nineteenth century). To this we can also add the appearance of the Aristotelianism that reached the Christian West through the Arabs.

Aristotle, in fact, in his masterly analysis of the act of knowledge, *demonstrates* [= *démontre* in French] that we know one thing by the concept we extract from it, whereas the Platonic doctrine *shows* [= *montre* in French] that true knowledge is an intuitive participation of intelligence in the essence of the

---

15 Such as the fourteenth-century hymn still sung today, *Ave verum Corpus*; *Christ the Original Mystery*, 416.

16 Cf. the papal bull *Unam sanctam* of Bonifacius VIII in 1302; *Christ the Original Mystery*, 417.

17 Émile Littré, Dictionnaire de la langue française (Paris: Hachette, 1880); *Christ the Original Mystery*, 419.

18 Elie Blanc, *Dict. de philosophie* (Lethielleux, 1906), col. 868; *Christ the Original Mystery*, 425.

known object (wisdom, *sapientia*, derived from *sapere*, to taste). Even if those doctrines are not mutually exclusive, it is clear that the Aristotelian trend and its nominalist drift will lead to the denial of any possibility of gnosis (as onto-logical knowledge) in favor of a simple (and simplistic) rationality. And so, even if in rough outline, this new noetic paradigm radicalizes the triple dichotomy of knowing and being, science and faith, and intellect and prayer. The perfect illustration of this (partial) paradigm is that a perfect atheist could be a perfect theologian, for theology has no need of the sacred in its intellectual operations![19]

The direct consequence, in any case, is that the mystical becomes the last possible locus of the Platonic noesis, with the risk of appearing — in the criticism of Aristotelian intellectualism or of the scientific rationality of nominalism — idealistic, even illuminist or supernaturalist.

However, it would be a mistake to consider among the mystics — the major ones in any case — only the psychologizing of internal states (even if St. Teresa of Avila, for example, adheres almost exclusively to psychological and subjective criteria to discern the different states of prayer) or the reduction of the spiritual life to passively experienced extraordinary phenomena.

While it is true that the account of a spiritual experience should not be a theological treatise, what remains is that the properly spiritual capacity of the intellect, its ontological value and the central place it occupies in the mystical life are indisputably documented in the mystical writings of St. John of the Cross (1542–1592), for example, writings which are inherently dogmatic and biblical-liturgical. So many masters such as Meister Eckhart (and also St. John of the Cross) never speak directly about their experiences and always express themselves objectively, in their full possession of a comprehensive philosophical and theological culture.

From the seventeenth to the mid-twentieth century an important debate about the distinction between acquired contemplation (human efforts) and infused contemplation (grace of God) presided over discussions on mysticism. With hindsight, it seems that this same change in the noetic system (from Platonism to Aristotelianism) has also led to the replication of such a distinc-tion. Indeed, since contemplation is "a simple intuition of the divine truth,"[20]

---

19 Cf. Luther, for example.

20 St. Thomas Aquinas, *Summa Theologiae* II-II, q. 180, a. 3; *Christ the Original Mystery*, 437.

from the theological point of view which prevails here, it is always the divine Object that defines the act by which It is seen. It is the Christic revelation (scriptural, liturgical and dogmatic) that actualizes and informs the intellect's innate contemplativity.

Similarly, in the traditional designation *ascetical and mystical theology*, both terms are related to a single 'way of perfection', in order to distinguish them from the 'moral life'. This distinction loses its meaning when applied to contemplation itself, either to divide it into various stages, or to infer from it an opposition between a "true active approach" and a "false passive approach." [21]

"The moral virtues are not concerned with the contemplative life in its essence," which is "consideration of the truth." However, they are concerned with it as a "disposition to this contemplative life."[22] Surely, God is free with his Gift (which is Himself) and nothing is due to human activities that are at once necessary and useless. Thus, with this essential and universal paradox, the synergistic unity between the ascetic and the mystical is constantly vouched for: St. Gregory of Nyssa, St. Dionysius, St. Augustine, St. Albert the Great, St. Thomas Aquinas, St. Bonaventure, Meister Eckhart, Tauler, Suso, St. Teresa of Avila, and St. John of the Cross, among others.

To conclude, we will stress one last and just as artificial hindrance, which consists in opposing the path of gnosis (of a Shankara) to the way of love (St. John of the Cross).[23] Actually, for St. John of the Cross (often misunderstood in this case), just as for accepted definitions like the following ones from St. Thomas Aquinas, "the last and crowning act is the contemplation itself of the truth,"[24] "the purity of the intelligible truth."[25] Likewise, "the intellectual act of theological contemplation gives rise to love in the soul and beauty pertains to its essence."[26]

21 Cf. René Guénon, *Initiation and Spiritual Realization*, 99; *Christ the Original Mystery*, 439.
22 St. Thomas Aquinas, *Summa Theologiae* II-II, q. 180, a. 2; *Christ the Original Mystery*, 439, n. 3.
23 Cf. Georges Vallin, *Voie de gnose et voie d'amour. Éléments de mystique comparée* (Paris: Ed. Présence, 1980); *Christ the Original Mystery*, 443.
24 St. Thomas Aquinas, *Summa Theologiae* II-II, q. 180, a. 3; *Christ the Original Mystery*, 441.
25 St. Thomas Aquinas, *Summa Theologiae* II-II, q. 180, a. 5; *Christ the Original Mystery*, 441.
26 Ibid., a. 2., reply to objection 3; *Christ the Original Mystery*, 441.

Moreover, to say that Christianity does not have a path of knowledge
as pure and radical as the *Vedanta*, for instance, when Christ is specifically
"the Way, the Truth and the Life," is to forget that, for a Christian, Christ is
by 'nature' or 'essence' knowledge of the Father, the incarnate *Logos*, and, as
we have already seen, the Truth. Setting aside this basic fact, integral to the
Christian path, is simply to no longer speak of Christianity itself.

FIVE

The Metaphysics of Analogy

Analogy, which binds together two 'things' through the relationship between them, bears a strong resemblance to a symbol, itself a link between something visible and something invisible. Analogy is not, for all that, a symbol. In fact, it is by assuming sensible forms that analogy becomes a symbol; and it is when "the symbol [is] deciphered [that it] is transformed into the analogy out of which it was made.... While the symbol can conceal analogy ... analogy offers the key for the symbol," it is "the sense of the symbol." [1]

In this way analogy brings us from the logical to the ontological and, beyond, leads us to the meontological (the meta-ontological) which is its basis (cf. chap. 7).

In his Penser l'analogie, *Jean Borella sweeps through the entire history of analogy. Of course we understand its mathematical source and its origin and use in logic, but we quickly arrive at the essential question of the analogy of being: in what way is man, when God is, above all when He declares: "I am who I am"? What then can this analogy be that would connect an existing creature with the Being who caused it? This question is treated in reverse chronological order: first, according to modern scholasticism (Jacques Maritain, R. Garrigou-Lagrange, etc.) with reference to Aristotle and the body of commentary that has followed him; next, according to St. Thomas Aquinas, especially in going back to his source, the Dionysian tradition; and finally, according to the Platonic doctrine of analogy, a true method "put to use for the resolution of the most essential questions of metaphysics."* [2] *These are the elements presented in this chapter.*

PHILOSOPHIC QUESTIONS, AT LEAST ACCORDING
to the Platonic way, dealing with being or essence (the thing in itself), should
not, when analogy is involved, be limited to analogy's simple relationship with

---

1 *Penser l'analogie,* 209.
2 Ibid., 19.

logic. In particular, beyond the famous reasoning 'by analogy' of scholasticism, there is the use made of this by symbolic thought. The former is based on the logical nature of analogy (as an operation of the mind), the latter on its ontological nature (as a property of the real).[3]

The 'logic of comparison' enables us to have some knowledge of what would remain otherwise unknown, such as the impulse of the nerves compared to the pulse of the blood, even though, *ontologically*, the being of the blood is unrelated to the being of nervous impulses. By contrast, in the physical order, comparing the wing of a bird with the fin of a fish, evolutionism will ask: might not the one be derived ontologically from the other? This ontological question is so much the more crucial in metaphysics where, between the principial Invisible and the natural visible, there are posited "relationships not only of similarity (and dissimilarity), but also of causality, and [the claim] that the effect necessarily participates, in some respects, in its cause."[4]

The Sources of Analogy

The Greek word *analogia* combines the multiple meanings of *logos* (discourse, word, thought, notion, reason, relationship) with the three principal themes of the meanings of *ana*:

- elevation: 'from below to above'
- return 'backwards' or 'in the opposite direction'
- repetition: 'once again'

Combined in *analogia*, we therefore have a "relationship (*logos*) between what is above and what is below (verticality), because what is below is like what is above (repetition) with, potentially, the idea of a reversal (the smallest as analogue of the greatest)."[5]

The direct transfer of *analogia* into Latin has ended up giving it the vague sense of a simple 'relationship', which must be completed by *comparatio* or *proportio*, until *proportio* becomes equivalent to 'proportional to', and Boethius

---

3 Ibid., 11.
4 Ibid., 13.
5 Ibid., 23.

is constrained to add again *proportionalitas* to express the mathematical sense of *analogia*: $a/b = c/d$.

In Greek literature before Plato the implicit doctrine associated with *analogia* is that of worlds open to one another (the supreme One, cycles, degrees of reality . . .), in such a way that *correspondences* and *comparisons* are possible. Akin to metaphor among the poets (Homer, Hesiod . . .), one can speak of *literary analogy*, as opposed to a *scientific* or *explicative analogy*. This last one, applied to natural phenomena, by which the known explains the unknown, will be termed *mechanical* or *physical*; applied to the knowledge of being and first principles, it will be called *philosophical* or *metaphysical analogy*.

SCIENTIFIC OR EXPLICATIVE ANALOGY	Philosophical or metaphysical analogy	Knowledge of being and first principles
	Mechanical or physical analogy	Natural phenomena
LITERARY ANALOGY	(correspondences, comparisons, metaphors)	Literature, Poetry

Empedocles (490–430 B.C.) is the Presocratic who made the greatest use of scientific analogy, showing, through nearly a hundred analogies (ear-seashell, embryo-seed, woman-moon, leaf-hair, universe-egg, etc.), that analogy is even more a revealer of the unifying presence of the One across the multiplicity of orders, that analogy is the research method for knowing the invisible starting with the visible.[6]

The origins of *analogia* also appear among the mathematicians of the Pythagorean school, such as Archytas of Tanentum (430–360 B.C.) who, in his *Treatise on Music*, distinguishes 3 medieties or means: arithmetical, geometrical and subcontrary (or harmonic). Considering a series of numbers such that $a < b < c$: In arithmetical mediety, the largest term exceeds the mean of the same quantity as the mean exceeds the smallest ($c - b = b - a$, such as with 1, 2, 3 or 2, 4, 6). In geometrical mediety the first term is to the second what the second is to the third ($a/b = b/c = b - a/c - b$, such as with 1, 2, 4 or 1, 3, 9). This is the only 'proportion' (*analogia*) in the proper sense: repetition (*ana*) of the same relationship (*logos*).

- harmonic mediety (as well as the seven others enumerated by Nicomachus of Gerasa) is less directly tied to the subject. One can write $b - a / c - b = a/c$. This is concerned with series such that 3, 4, 6 or 6, 8, 12 are utilized in harmony or in the geometry of solids (the cube, for example, having 6 sides, 8 vertices, 12 edges).[7]

MEDIETY	DEFINITION	FORMULA	EXAMPLES
ARITHMETICAL	*the largest term exceeds the mean of the same quantity as the mean exceeds the smallest*	$c - b = b - a$	1, 2, 3 2, 4, 6
GEOMETRICAL	*the first term is to the second what the second is to the third*	$a/b = b/c$	1, 2, 4 1, 3, 9
HARMONIC	*the quotient of the difference between the mean term and the smallest and the largest and the mean is equal to the quotient of the large term over the small*	$(b-a)/(c-b)$ $= a/c$	3, 4, 6 6, 8, 12

Analogy of Proportionality and Analogy of Attribution

Especially because interest in analogy has been considerably rekindled in the course of the 20th century, it seems appropriate, not to follow the chronology of the philosopheme such as the history of philosophy might do (with good reason), but to start with the problematic as posed by modern philosophers, insofar as this question is basically always relevant, seeing that "the nature of analogy is concerned with the very possibility of metaphysical knowledge."[8]

The point of departure for the modern period is the standard doctrine of analogy in modern scholasticism as still taught at the beginning of the 20th century. Scholasticism informs us of two types of analogy according to Aristotle: analogy of proportionality and analogy of 'attribution'.

- **Analogy of proportionality**, initially mathematical ($a/b = c/d$), shows a relationship of equality or identity between two relationships: *a* is to *b* what *c* is to *d*. Beyond its original domain, we could offer an example such as "the wing is to the bird what the fin is to the fish,"

---

7 Ibid., 26–28.
8 Ibid., 32.

or else "sight is to the eye what intellection is to the soul," or again "the lion is to animals what the king is to men." Hence, a *metaphoric analogy* (the lion is the king of animals) will be distinguished from an *analogy of proportionality proper* (the seeing of the eye is a true knowledge, just as intellection is).

ANALOGY OF PROPORTIONALITY	EXAMPLES
FOR PROPORTIONALITY PROPER	*Sight is to the eye what intellection is to the soul*
METAPHORICAL	*The lion is to the animals what the king is to men*
MATHEMATICAL	a/b = c/d

- **Analogy of attribution** is the mode according to which one *same* term is *attributed* to two different entities in neither univocal nor equivocal fashion. A univocal attribution would be, for example, the word *animal*, which is said of a dog in the same sense that it is said of a man; an equivocal attribution would be, for example, the name *dog*, which does not have the same meaning if this involves a different animal or a constellation of the same name. What is decisive is that, besides the univocal meaning and the absence of meaning (an equivocal meaning being in fact a non-meaning), there exists an intermediate meaning: to be precise, the analogical meaning. The classical example derived from Aristotle is the adjective 'healthy', attributed just as legitimately to an animal, a remedy, a drink, or urine. 'Healthy' is attributed to the animal in the proper sense, to a remedy by reason of its active cause, to a drink as a preserving cause and to urine by reason of a sign.

ANALOGY OF ATTRIBUTION			
SIGN	Urine		
PRESERVING CAUSE	Drink	healthy	Analogical attribution
ACTIVE CAUSE	Remedy		
PROPER SENSE	Animal		

Univocal attribution	Animal	Man	
		Dog	Dog
		Constellation	Equivocal attribution

In the analogical mode of attribution, reference is always made to a primary entity, the 'principal analogate', in which the term has its full 'real' meaning. Meaning is attributed *per prius* (by priority) to this analogate; to the others it is attributed *per posterius* (posteriorly or secondarily) and these are therefore 'secondary analogates'.[9]

For these secondary analogates the analogy of attribution does not have exactly the same meaning, depending on how it is viewed: The analogical relationship they maintain among themselves on the basis of their *common* relationship with the primary analogate is spoken of, then, as a relationship *plurium ad unum* (of several in relationship with a single one) or *duorum ad tertium* (of two terms with respect to a third), for the relationship they maintain among themselves (healthy drink and healthy urine, for example) makes sense only as a function of their relationship to the primary analogate (the healthy animal, in this example). The relationship that each secondary analogate, taken separately, maintains with the primary one — which relationship establishes the others — is, on the other hand, spoken of as an *unius ad alterum* relationship.

ANALOGY OF ATTRIBUTION IN SECONDARY ANALOGATES			
	Health	*plurium ad unum*	*unius ad alterum*
Secondary analogates *Meaning attributed per posterius*	**Urine**		
	Drink		
	Remedy		
Primary analogate *Meaning attributed per prius*	**Animal**		

What remains is to distinguish that 'extrinsic' analogy of attribution (health is never attributed formally and really to secondary analogates) from cases where "one same term is attributed to different realities while formally retaining, to a certain extent, the same meaning . . . [designating then] a property intrinsic to each of the entities to which it is attributed, whether this involves a primary analogate or secondary ones."[10]

By saying that "quality is (exists), quantity is (exists)," we attribute being to these two categories as an intrinsic property — this is even their unique common point — enabling them to be introduced into a relationship of

9 Ibid., 34.
10 Ibid., 35.

analogy. For all that, neither quality nor quantity possesses being by itself. This is what the example of the clover will illustrate: it itself exists, but neither the quantity 'three' (its number of leaves) nor the quality 'green' (its color) can be encountered as such. It will be said that these are *accidents* (green, three) of a *substance* (clover) and that they exist only in proportion to the attribution of being to substance. And the order of the attribution of being is thus, as previously, either *per prius* (the clover) or *per posterius* (three, green).

But — and this is what is decisive — the analogy of attribution signifies this order of attribution itself. It "expresses this *ontological law* that, in reality, there is not a pure fusion of the multiple into the unity of a monolithic being, nor a pure spread or dissemination of being into a multiplicity of entities and unrelated to one another, but a *hierarchy of relationship with 'participation' in being.*"[11]

Analogy of Being can be said to be Aristotelian

The denial of any analogical unity of being in Aristotle rests on the conviction that being is for him an unresolved problem and is recognized as such, an aporia: an insurmountable difficulty.

"Aristotelian philosophy holds that there is, in fact, a not purely homonymic plurality of acceptations of being diversified according to categories, and yet, since not a genus, it should not be present, according to the identity of its signification, in diverse categories (as is for example the genus 'animal', identical in man and oxen). If therefore it does not possess the identity of a genus, without losing for all that its (relative) unity of signification, how do we think about it? This is why we can speak of an 'ontology of the impossible'. As for theology, it is 'pointless' to think about ontology because, even though theology gains God, the first Act of Being, eternal and separated Substance, it loses the being of things with which the first Act of Being has no relationship, the being of things which should however be taken into account."[12]

---

11 Ibid., 36. [Editor's emphasis]

12 Ibid., 57–8. According to Paul Ricœur, "an aporetic interpretation of Aristotelian ontology . . . over-dramatizes the encounter between an 'ontology of the impossible' — for want of a thinkable unity between the categories — and a 'theology of the useless' — for want of an assignable relationship between the God that thinks Himself and the world He is unaware of." *La métaphore vive* (Paris: Seuil, 1975), 331, note 1.

If the only manner of existing is that of an individual substance, *accidents* do not have "the being that it is nevertheless necessary to attribute to them, ontology is not to be found and theology is of no use: being is impartible, being each time incommunicably possessed by each individual substance, and by God, the first of all."[13]

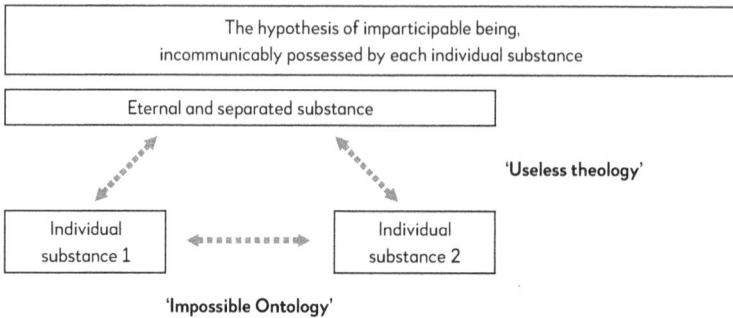

However, besides this 'ontology of individual substance' which corresponds to an objective aspect of Aristotelianism and is opposed to the analogy of being, there is in Aristotle a whole other and complementary ontology, that of act and potency. It might even be said that "his 'vision of the real' oscillates between an ontology (of substance and accidents) and an energology (of act and potency) . . . [which is to say] that it possesses, by fidelity to the real, certain more-or-less conciliable tensions; hence its wondrous fecundity."[14]

This distinction of act and potency is a major discovery of Aristotle's philosophy: for a being to pass from what is in potency to what is in act is to become what it has for being, to realize its nature, and therefore to go towards more perfection and more being (for example, the eye attains its perfection of being when it exercises its act of seeing). Thus, insofar as it was first in potency, every being in act has become so through another being in act so that:

- "the property of act is to communicate its actuality . . . [and]
- every act of whatever is in potency is a secondary act that supposes a first act."[15] And "without an absolutely first act, nothing would

13 *Penser l'analogie*, 58.
14 Ibid., 58–9.
15 Ibid., 59–60.

be really in act. It follows that this first Act is also First Being, the Being absolutely being, namely God."[16]

Here is where the ontological barrier which separates accident from substance is crossed: accident is the secondary act of what is actuated first in substance. Accidents can reveal only what was perforce already in potency in substance. Hence accidents are no longer "a collection of determinations in substance: inasmuch as they are secondary acts of a first act, they are unified by this very act, they are, says Aristotle, its *analogon*."[17]

Moreover, theology should not be "the grave of ontology: interpreted as energology, it is to the contrary its unique condition of possibility. . . . The universality of being (the fact that it can be said of all things) is only explicable as a consequence of the primacy of Divine Being."[18] Without this theology of the pure Act of First Being, the universality of being would only be an abstraction and ontology would be reduced to logic, whereas "it is a metaphysics of act which ultimately substitutes itself . . . for the logic of being."[19]

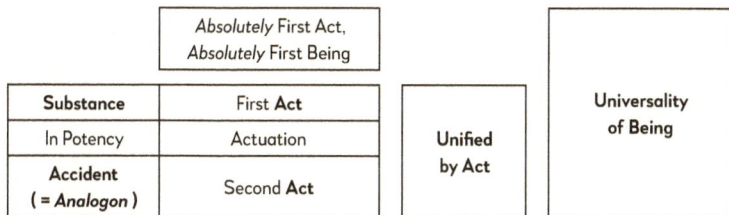

	Absolutely First Act, Absolutely First Being		
Substance	First Act		**Universality of Being**
In Potency	Actuation	**Unified by Act**	
Accident (= Analogon)	Second **Act**		

On this basis the analogy of being is possible in Aristotelian philosophy, even if it will be left to St. Thomas Aquinas to go to the end of this metaphysic.[20]

16 Ibid., 61.

17 *Metaphysics* VIII, 2, 1043a5; *Penser l'analogie*, 60.

18 *Penser l'analogie*, 61.

19 Christian Rutten, "L'analogie chez Aristote," *Revue de philosophie ancienne*, 1983, n°1, 48; *Penser l'analogie*, 61.

20 *Penser l'analogie*, 62.

Aquinian Analogy of Being

It is in the *Summa*[21] that St. Thomas will formulate the doctrine of analogy of being, which will express, in addition to a logic of the attribution of names, an ontology of participation. To do this it would be necessary to hold, on the one hand, that the being attributed to God and creatures is no longer conceived of as a third something common to both and, on the other, that the participation of creatures in the being attributed to God "takes into account precisely their distinction from the Uncreated and their ordering on the ladder of beings with respect to First Being."[22] The first condition is acquired when St. Thomas gains access to the concept of being as an 'act of being' (*actus essendi*); the second when the biblical notion of creation *ex nihilo*, which "is the donation of all being, that is, not only of the nature or essence of the creature but also of its existing as such in its most complete actuality 'out of nothing' (*ex nihilo*) . . . not a statically constituted difference, but a differentiation in act and always acting . . . a continual sallying forth out of nothingness."[23]

Hence, being as act (*esse*) is not a something (*ens*), not a metaphysical form which would be combined from without with the thing — being would then be an accident — but, ungraspable, it is not the thing itself but its actuality, the fact that it really exists. Neither the form nor essence of a thing, not even its substance, is the being of this thing, "but being (*être, esse*) is that by which substance is called a being (*étant, ens*)."[24]

The *esse* is thus at once exterior to the nature of the creature and "what is most intimate and most profoundly inherent to it"; it becomes equally possible to attribute it to God, where, not being a something, He can be participated in by creatures — participation in the Act of divine being: "there

21 Two Aquinian approaches, which are not presented in this summary, precede this analogy of being ultimately formulated in the *Summa*: one that ends with an applicability to the transcendental analogy of 'the analogy of similarity' (of deficient similarity) and which Thomas developed initially in the *Commentary on the Book of Sentences*; and one that ends with a (merely logical) applicability of the 'analogy of proportionality', developed further in *De Veritate*. The table shown at the end of the article summarizes these stages of Aquinian reflection [French editor's note].

22 *Penser l'analogie*, 76.

23 Ibid., 77.

24 St. Thomas Aquinas, *Contra Gentiles*, II, 54; *Penser l'analogie*, 80.

can be a proportion of the creature to God, inasmuch as it is related to Him as the effect to its cause, and as potentiality to its act."²⁵

What the creature's act of being actualizes ultimately is one of any number of incompatible natures ('man', 'tree', 'cat'...); in God, the essence is pure actuality of being, it is a 'pure act of being' (*actus purus essendi*), limitless, infinite. Thus, being is common to Creator and creatures but, at the same time, infinitely different "since, for the creature, being is to receive the participation of God's infinite Act of being into the finiteness of its essence."²⁶ This participation therefore bespeaks deficiency but, at the same time, resemblance: "the resemblance of something to its causal agent happens through the act since the agent produces its likeness insofar as it is in act."²⁷ It is this "efficient causality by which God confers on creatures participation in His Act of being, which unites them to Him just as much as It distinguishes them from Him," and this conception of efficient causality "as the gift of participation in the divine Act of being takes into account both divine immanence and divine transcendence."²⁸ Moreover, "the analogical relationship of the created to the Uncreated is henceforth grasped in its *reality* as an ontological ordering of the one to the Other, and no longer as an expediency simply logical in nature."²⁹

This analogy of being—it is through analogy that there is analogy between the creature and God—enables us to breach, with the same stroke, the Aristotelian barrier between the Infinite and the finite, which St. Thomas had respected at one time (*De Veritate*). Moreover, the act being what the effect has in common with its cause as well as what distinguishes it, "creative causality establishes between beings and God the indispensable link of participation so that there may be an analogy of relationship between them,"³⁰ classically named analogy of attribution.

25 St. Thomas Aquinas, *Summa theologiae*, I, q. 12, a. 1; *Penser l'analogie*, 82.
26 *Penser l'analogie*, 81.
27 *Contra Gentiles*, II, 53; *Penser l'analogie*, 81.
28 *Penser l'analogie*, 82.
29 Ibid., 84.
30 Bernard Montagnes, *La doctrine de l'analogie de l'être d'après saint Thomas d'Aquin* (Paris: Ed. du Cerf, 2008), 91–2; *Penser l'analogie*, 83.

Thus the question of differentiating between analogy of proportionality or analogy of attribution has lost its importance and the *unius ad alterum* analogy, initially retained by Thomas (*Commentary on the Book of Sentences*), then rejected (*De Veritate*), has become again, thanks to the analogy of the act of being, the only possible one: "There can be two manners of analogy. On the one hand, depending on whether several things are related to a single one [*plurium ad unum*, with reference to the example about health]. On the other, depending on whether one has regard, not for the order or relationship of two things to a third [*duorum ad tertium*], but for the relationship of one of two things to the other [*unius ad alterum*]: thus, 'being' (*ens*) is said about substance and accident, depending on whether accident has a relationship with substance, and not depending on whether substance and accident would relate to a third something. Consequently, for the names attributed to God and to other beings, they are said, not according to the first mode (which would imply that one could posit something before God), but according to the second mode."[31]

STAGES	TYPE OF ANALOGY	APPLICABILITY TO TRANSCENDENTAL ANALOGY
I. *Commentary on the Book of Sentences* (Prol., q.1, a.2, arg. 2)	Analogy "by reference to a first": *plurium ad unum* or *duorum ad tertium*	Inapplicable: no third term common to God and man
	unius ad alterum (analogy of similarity)	Applicable: "deficient similarity"
II. *De Veritate* (q.2, a.11)	Relationship between things: *unius ad alterum*	Inapplicable *logically*: no relationship possible between the Infinite and the finite
	Relationship between relationships (analogy of proportionality)	Applicable *logically* but a non-ontological analogy
III. *Summas* (*Contra Gentiles, De Potentia, Summa Theologiae . . .*)	*plurium ad unum, duorum ad tertium*	Inapplicable: no third term common to God and man
	Analogy of the act of being *unius ad alterum* (analogy of attribution)	Applicable *ontologically*: Ontological ordering of the created to the Uncreated

---

31 St. Thomas Aquinas, *Contra Gentiles*, I, 34; *Penser l'analogie*, 84.

Dionysian Analogy

The "risk of univocity could be formulated in this way: how are we to account for the multiplicity of beings if they all participate in the same unique Act of divine being?" We must therefore discern in what this participation in the Act of divine being consists and what it effects in the creature.

- It is the creature's essence that limits the act of being because it is something with a particular essence and not the act of being as such. From this point of view, essence seems to be "a lessening, a stretching and, as it were, a scattering of Being . . . a spare change of Being."[32] What we have here is the 'existentialist' Gilsonian interpretation of the Aquinian *esse*: essence limits the act of being, preventing it from attaining the fullness of perfection, whereas in God no essence limits the act of being (one might say in this sense that God has no essence, but St. Thomas prefers to say that "His essence is nothing but His being":[33] His essence being made up of being, it should in no way limit this act). We are dealing with an analogy of proportionality here. The relationship of the *esse* to the essence of a single being having been conceived, it is valid for all beings x, y and z: the essence of x / the existence of x = the essence of y / the existence of y = the essence of z / the existence of z. Hence the multiplicity of beings is unified only according to the identity of their essence/existence relationship, and each being is posited next to other beings, isolated by its own essence. In addition, this multiplicity is irreducible, with each essence reduced to being only a pure potency to receive the act of being.

- There is another aspect of Thomistic thought where essences are, in addition to being pure powers of receptivity to the act of being, similitudes of the divine perfections such as they are in God's

---

32 Etienne Gilson, *Introduction à la philosophie chrétienne* (Vrin, 1969), 173 and 192; cf. Bernard Montagnes, *La doctrine de l'analogie de l'être d'après saint Thomas d'Aquin*, 161; *Penser l'analogie*, 120.

33 Thomas d'Aquin, Dietrich de Freiberg, *L'Étant et l'Essence. Le vocabulaire médiéval de l'ontologie*, trans. & commentary by Alain de Libera et Cyrille Michon (Paris: Points-Seuil, 1996); *De ente et essentia*, V, 1, 107; *Penser l'analogie*, 120.

Essence. In fact, "the Divine Essence contains in Itself all possible perfections under the form of eternal Ideas, identical to God (in God all is God), which are so many modes according to which the Divine Essence allows Itself to be participated in by creatures."[34] The Divine Essence viewed as an infinity of perfections is a doctrine that St. Thomas has not found explicitly in Aristotle, but in the Platonic tradition and foremost in St. Dionysius the Areopagite. St. Thomas will formulate that this infinite Perfection tends to communicate itself by very virtue of its Goodness: *Bonum diffusivum sui esse* (the Good is diffusive of its being) by expressly summarizing the thought of St. Dionysius. Hence "the entire *order* of creation results from the irradiation of infinite Perfection participated in, according to the modes of a necessarily deficient similarity, by the essence of each creature."[35] This essence being a mode of divine Perfection, with this mode it becomes possible to know something of the divine Perfection Itself.

Moreover, the sum total of these essences forms then a hierarchical order of the degrees of these perfections: more sheer multiplicity, but a multiplicity ordered in relation to a principle.

"These degrees of perfections, which are also and necessarily degrees of being, are distributed from the lowest to the loftiest according to the Neoplatonic (and Patristic) hierarchy of being, life and knowledge. God, supreme Perfection, is being, life and knowledge in the simplicity of His Essence. All creatures participate in the perfection of being (as do the minerals); some add to being the perfection of life (plants and animals); lastly, some others add to the perfection of life that of intellectual knowledge (man and angelic creatures)." Moreover, within these degrees of essential perfections "we should distinguish modes which define so many secondary degrees of creaturely perfections, or particular forms of essential perfections. Thus there are three modes of perfection of knowledge: the sensible mode (common to animals and man), the rational mode (proper to man), and the angelic mode. As we see, the hierarchically ordered multiplicity of essences is not only unified

34 *Penser l'analogie*, 122.
35 Ibid., 124.

with respect to supreme Perfection, this is also so through the relationships that essences maintain among themselves."[36]

Essence does not receive existence properly speaking; it is the mode of actuation of the act of being, it is its determining principle according to the mode of perfection that defines its nature, depending on whether, therefore, it is a particular essence, similarity to a particular divine perfection, or, better said, a particular similarity to the unique and simple divine Perfection. And it is insofar as it is a deficient similarity of divine Perfection that it realizes an analogical manifestation of this Perfection. Analogy is not identical to participation; "it declares that this participation is measured, it enunciates this very measure, and by that establishes the analogy of being, which means that it accounts for the analogical character of being when it is attributed to both God and creature, since it is it (the analogy) that 'modalizes' its infinite and pure Actuality."[37]

"Analogy thus appears to be the 'place' of the unity and distinction of essence and existence . . . *ontology is basically analogical because the reality of a creature is basically defined as an analogy. And even more than analogical, being is revealed to be **analogal***";[38] that is, not only does the human spirit introduce it into a relationship of participative similarity with the divine Exemplar, but it realizes in itself and through itself such a relationship.

And it is with St. Dionysius the Areopagite that "the 'analogality' of the creature is grasped in its most radical truth."[39]

The Dionysian *analogia* designates "the measure according to which the divine similitude is participated in by creatures: it is the measure of likeness, of the theomorphism of creatures."[40] It is in God who fixes the measure according to which He confers His likeness on creatures and in creatures as a property of their being.

- The divine *analogia* is identified with the Platonic Idea, with what Dionysius calls *paradeigma*: model; "we call models the divine

36 Ibid., 125–6.
37 Ibid., 126–7.
38 Ibid., 127.
39 Ibid.
40 Ibid., 128.

creative reasons of essences, which pre-exist the latter in unity."[41]

- The *analogia* of the creature, the measure of the likeness, is a gift of God which is only fulfilled if the gift is related to the Giver, "to the extent of our spiritual generosity and our love."[42]

The logical or mathematical connotation of analogy is integral to the ontological constitution of the beings of creation: a measure measured out in creatures, a measure measuring in God. Above all, beyond the late distinction between analogies of proportionality and attribution, the Dionysian *analogia* reveals that "what there is of the true in proportionality (and which results from the cosmic distribution of one same *logos*) and what there is of the true in attribution (and which results from ontological participation according to a deficient similarity) are conjoined in the theophanic mystery of creation."[43]

Analogy therefore expresses the link that attaches the creature to its Principle. Through this analogy God is in the creature and the creature is in God, insofar as it measure the distance which, while separating them, unites them.

Still more generally, analogy teaches us that being is relationship and that relationship is being:

- in God, in the Trinitarian mystery where the persons are subsistent relationships, and the relationships persons, and
- in creation, where the very being of the creature is *analogia*, a relationship of ontological dependence on the Creator.

"However, even though analogy reveals to us this dual face of the real, it does not enable us to intelligently delve into its mysterious and transcendent unity; and no human intelligence can surpass here the ultimate duality of the aspects under which the real is given to us."[44]

---

41 *Des Noms divins*, *P.G.*, tome III, 824c; Roques, *L'univers dionysien*, 62; *Penser l'analogie*, 129.

42 Roques, 63; *Penser l'analogie*, 129.

43 *Penser l'analogie*, 131.

44 Ibid., 132.

CAVE AND ANALOGY

Sophists have proven themselves destructive of any analogicity by proposing a pure appearance totally disconnected from being. On the other hand, the analogy, 'the most beautiful of links', measures the distance from appearance to being, from the model to its image, from the Invisible to the visible, from the intelligible archetype to its sensible presence. For the sophist, contrary to the Parmenidean paralysis that joined *logos* to being, word and being are seen to differ. However, the real remedy for these two biases "is analogy which speaks simultaneously of difference and unity, identity and otherness." And this analogical distance between being and appearance does not only apply to the order of discourse, it also applies to the order of reality.[45]

In the final pages of Book 6 and in the first of Book 7 of the *Republic*, "Plato, for the first time in the history of philosophical thought, expressly applies the notion of analogy to the resolution of the most fundamental metaphysical questions. . . . Here we have an exemplary demonstration of 'dialectic power'. . . [applied] to the revelation of cosmic *mimesis*, since every being is the image of a higher reality to which it refers, until finally, from analogy to analogy, we ascend, if possible, to the Supreme Good."[46] Plato essentially introduces three cases of analogical structure:

- The first is the Idea of the Good, beyond being and essence, with "what the Good has engendered as its sensory analogue."
- To the second structure is related the representation of the degrees of reality and levels of knowledge in the form of a vertical line divided by geometric proportionality, the only 'proportion' (*analogia*) properly speaking: a repetition (*ana*) of the same rapport (*logos*).
- The third is the famous 'allegory' of the cave itself: "a complex picture of analogic structure in a symbolic guise."

The first structure will be presented in Chapter 7. As for the second one, the mathematico-philosophical 'line', here are the key points:

---

45 *Penser l'analogie*, 163.
46 Ibid.

- Its division by geometrical proportionality allows us to obtain 4 segments a, b, c and d with a + b / c + d = a/b = c/d where b = c.[47]

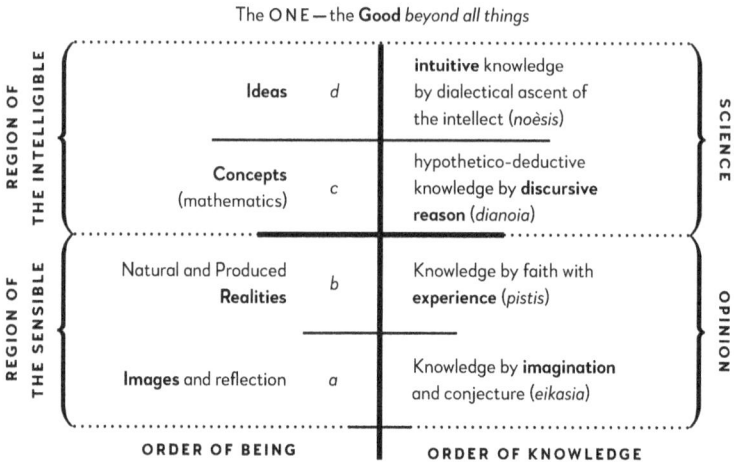

The O N E — the **Good** *beyond all things*

REGION OF THE INTELLIGIBLE	**Ideas**	d	**intuitive** knowledge by dialectical ascent of the intellect (*noèsis*)	SCIENCE
	Concepts (mathematics)	c	hypothetico-deductive knowledge by **discursive reason** (*dianoia*)	
REGION OF THE SENSIBLE	Natural and Produced **Realities**	b	Knowledge by faith with **experience** (*pistis*)	OPINION
	Images and reflection	a	Knowledge by **imagination** and conjecture (*eikasia*)	

ORDER OF BEING   **ORDER OF KNOWLEDGE**

- Contrary to what many commentators have argued, the first segment seems remarkable because it "makes clear that there is in sensory reality, in the sensitive being, however obviously and indisputably full of the non-real, the apparent and the illusory it may be... an image and therefore a model." From the corporeal "the world resonates on itself and redoubles itself... the most humble, the lowest degree of reality reveals the analogical structure of the real and invites us to our own transcendence... no reality of the sensitive world can be 'taken literally'.... Being is not only 'absolute', but also 'relationship.'"[48]
- This is also true for the Ideas, the highest degree of reality, with the exception of the Idea of a One-Good that is no longer a degree. However, "we can understand analogy in the sense of a climb to the top: the reflection, the shadow, the image appeal to the model, the paradigm, the exemplar. But why should there be a shadow or a reflection? Why is the splendor of Ideas not self-sufficient?"[49]

47 This equality of the two intermediate segments (c and b) is significant and relevant to the Platonic conception of mathematical knowledge, an aspect not covered here.

48 *Penser l'analogie*, 167.

49 Ibid., 168.

This is what the third analogical structure, the 'image' of the cave, should explain. While the Line deploys the "fundamental degrees of this dual analogy that unites the visible to the superintelligible by the mediation of a hierarchy of ontological levels", and provides "a complete metaphysical map of the degrees of reality and levels of knowledge that pertain to this Line," the Cave "falls within the order of being and its realization." We are no longer in "the objective and impersonal order of an abstract representation of reality, but the Cave locates the human being in his concrete condition taken as a starting point for the realization of this reality."[50]

"According to the faithful translation of the *Complete Works* of Plato that Leo Robin published in the *Bibliothèque de la Pléiade* . . . prisoners are chained to the bottom of a steep cave, their heads immobilized facing a wall. Behind them rises a road that is blocked, at a certain height, by a wall. Rising above the wall we can see artifacts, statues and effigies of living beings made of wood or stone carried by men hidden behind the wall, among whom some are speaking. Further up but *inside* the cave (otherwise it would have no effect) is a blazing fire whose light projects the shadows of the artifacts (an echoic kind of language) onto the back wall. Finally, right at the top, the cave opens wide to the outside. Basically, this is a shadow puppet theater."[51]

Furthermore, the myth comprises two parts:

- Once freed from their chains, when they finally reach the 'sun-light', the prisoners begin another *paideia* (training, education, initiation) but with progressively *real* realities: shadows, beings themselves, nocturnal contemplation of the stars, ending with the sun itself. This is therefore first a noetic deconditioning and then a reconditioning to another kind of knowledge. There is also a correspondence—indicated by Plato—between the exit from the Cave (and education in the open air) and the two parts of the line: the sensible and the intelligible.
- After having raised his eyes to the sun, the philosopher must come down to the bottom of the cave, with the risk of being killed when he reveals to the prisoners that they take shadows for reality (an

50 Ibid., 169.
51 Ibid., 169–70.

allusion to the death of Socrates). Compared to the line where the soul, having been elevated, finishes "its course towards the Ideas,[52] . . . the descent into the Cave is therefore no longer in the order of knowledge, but of existence: it is necessary for whoever cares to save people from their confinement in the prison of illusory knowledge."[53]

Even if we could think the contrary, it might seem that the second part of the myth (the open-air *paideia*) does not repeat the first (ascent from the Cave). Together, they constitute the course, the dialectical ascent, the metaphysical journey "related to the very being of the traveler, which brings him to 'birth,' or rather 'rebirth' in the light of Being,"[54] a grace that brings one from appearance to reality:

- In order to move from appearance to reality, we must realize "the *genesis of appearances*, because knowledge (*noesis*) always questions the reasons for things"; this is the role of the first part with its symbolic explanation of the shadows and the illusion that they entail. That is why the Cave exhibits an artificial device, fictitious to the second degree: a kind of 'mental experience' almost impossible to replicate. "The entire underground system is a symbol of the genesis of the sensible world, but an *artificial* symbol to signify the *theoretical* nature of this genetic explanation."[55]
- Hence, the second part describes the stages that lead to getting used to the light (that is to say the truth): initiation to metaphysical realities, based on the symbolism of natural things.

This is also why the Cave "is underground and therefore as if outside of the world; it is a *non-place* and a *non-time* only inhabited by our thoughts and, as such, only exists and dwells in our thoughts. . . . This is indeed the *situs* of any doctrine which is, like the logos that thinks it, in reality a non-reality. It is a kind of non-being. Being a view *into* and a speaking *about* reality — whether

52 *Republic*, VI, 511c.
53 *Penser l'analogie*, 171.
54 Ibid., 173.
55 Ibid., 174–75.

sensible or intelligible reality—metaphysical theory is distinct in being the *other* by which and in which the real is *illumined* and knows itself. This void in the real by which the real is illumined and in which consists the possibility of speculative knowledge is quite precisely, at the core of the mountain-stone's rocky fullness, the recess, the hollow of the Cave where shines the light of the science of being and appearance.

"The Cave-doctrine is the infra-world, the reverse analogue of the supra-world from which it originates: the extra-ontological possibility of the doctrinal *logos* is the inverse reflection of the supra-ontological light of the One-Good. . . . Obviously, the Cave-doctrine's 'outside of the world' points to the transcendence of its origin."[56]

It is also "the cave of our cranium under the vault of which is lit the light of our intelligence and the wall onto which are projected the shadows of our thoughts. And finally, synthetically and symbolically summarized, it is the very doctrine of Plato, which bestows the myth of the Cave on our own metaphysical imagination. An initiatory Cave assuredly, since it is, as myth, a seed-doctrine sown in our minds and by the grace of which we are initiated to the knowledge of reality."[57]

Therefore, we should not content ourselves with a 'speculative' realization that shows us the image of the cave. The spiritual act of intelligence which comprises this doctrine is already, "in its intrinsic reality, something supernatural and, at its inspiring root, a participatory and direct emanation of the infinite Light of God."[58] But "this is the man who thinks, not the intellect as such"; and the aim is not to "liberate the intellect, which is somehow already free, but [to] deliver man. So begins this new *paideia* in the sunlight." If Plato seems to repeat himself, this is because he shows, "with the help of the myth itself, that we must go beyond the myth." He demonstrates "the need to move from doctrine as theoretical representation to its actual implementation."[59]

The "innate sense of being or of the real that is in us, and which is presupposed by Plato throughout the Myth of the Cave," is one of the keys to the first two parts:

56 Ibid., 175–76.
57 Ibid., 176.
58 Ibid., 177.
59 Ibid.

- In the first, if the shadows, true to their models, allow for a 'conjectural'[60] knowledge, this is because "the mistake does not come from the shadows themselves, but from a *judgment* passed on the shadows by the prisoners." And "this judgment is extra-conceptual, it is involved in any affirmation of existence. . . . It is this sense of being" that is the cause of the illusion. "It is also this sense of reality (which is one with intelligence) that makes possible the salvation of the prisoner, since the (anonymous) initiator prompts a reaction at all stages of initiation."[61]
- In the second, this sense of being is clearly also "the inner guide of the ascent to the light. It is this guide that transforms and deepens the *paideia*, not in its essence, but in the awareness that the metaphysical traveler has of it as he becomes more and more closely attuned to the objects disclosed by his noetic ascent."[62]

One last point must be emphasized: What do the characters holding the figures behind the wall in the cave represent? We need to start again from the Ideas, which have two faces, one facing the cosmos and another one which is supra-cosmic:

- The metaphysical parable of the Cave teaches that the ideas take part in the formation of the cosmic drama. They provide the foundation needed for sensible appearances and are involved in the cosmogonic process. They are "realities for things and radiate in them through all levels of the cosmos, not as being-thing but as being-relation":[63] "Among the Ideas, for all those that are what they are only in their mutual relations, it is only in this relationship that they have their reality."[64] They are "archetypal relations, structuring matrices . . . both everywhere and nowhere." Their being is *paradigmatic*:[65] "They measure, define and compose all

---

60 *Republic*, VII, 516c–d; *Penser l'analogie*, 182.
61 *Penser l'analogie*, 182–83.
62 Ibid., 183.
63 Ibid., 184.
64 *Parmenides*, 133c; *Penser l'analogie*, 185.
65 Ideas "remain set up (*estanai*) as paradigms" (*Parmenides*, 132b–d).

the analogous relationships that hierarchically order the universe," by their face as turned to the cosmos.[66]

- As for their supra-cosmic face, it is even more elusive.

It is the distinction between these two faces or two levels of Ideas which is marked by the wall behind which are hidden the invisible characters. Indeed, in its length, the wall separates two regions of the Cave. In its height, the wall marks the difference between "what of the Essences is perceptible to the mind's eye" and "what, at a deeper level, remains hidden." The wall thus defines the separation — and the communication threshold between the two — between the cosmic and the supra-cosmic, the created and the uncreated, the manifested and the unmanifested. "There are essences in the world as paradigms of the cosmic structure, and there are Essences *in divinis* as 'principial possibilities' contained in the Divine Essence."[67]

The hidden characters symbolize therefore "the eidetic principles (hidden in the divine nature) of the cosmic paradigms at work in the constitution of the world . . . the uncreated essences are roots that demiurgically inform sensible realities. . . . In other words, they symbolize the immanence of the multiple in the One, the principial multiplicity of the ultimate reasons for all things. . . . This multiplicity or 'supreme relativity' is 'the real "place" of pure ideas,'" and in some respect could be "identified with the Word-Wisdom as the 'place of the possibles.'"[68]

And as for the fact that these characters are only encountered in the third part of the myth: the return descent, is, for Plato, the decisive 'spiritual lesson': "desire for the light of Being is the only reason that the prisoner moves towards the conversion that frees him from his chains, not the knowledge of the mystery of the multiplicity of things which he must instead, in some way, progressively renounce."[69]

And so, "when engaged in the way of realization, the only focus of the metaphysician must be absolute and unconditioned Being (Sun-Good) and *not the knowledge of the multiple's reason for being*. Such knowledge is hidden in God Himself. It is the true secret of God and His creative irradiation. Any

---

66 *Penser l'analogie*, 185.

67 Ibid., 185–86.

68 Ibid., 175–88.

69 Ibid., 188.

who would set for themselves that knowledge as a goal could only reach it by halting their ascent to the good and turning away from the light of the principle. They would lose themselves permanently, believing that they had unlocked the secrets of creation when they were actually and thoroughly prisoners of illusion."[70] To enter into this super-knowledge, the Pauline 'epignosis', they must "have renounced all knowledge, even the knowledge of Ideas."[71]

This means that "the metaphysical intelligence must be involved in a concrete manner in faith in the revealed God: without revelation, no divine Subject"; "and without the divine Subject . . . no possible deliverance, since any pilgrimage towards an absent light is precluded. The intelligence must effect a kind of *sacrificium intellectus*. It must be buried in the faith as well as in the death of Christ-*Logos* in order to be reborn with him."[72]

This sense of Platonic dialectics and of the doctrine of Ideas was not understood by Aristotle, who conceived of being under the form of the existence of a thing, of an individual substance. Having said that, what would be the interest of those intelligible 'things', unnecessarily doubling the world of sensible realities? If Ideas are rather the relational matrices and unifying principles of any degree of reality, they are then independent of any degree of determined being. Wonderfully free, they thereby save multiplicity from its own annihilating dispersal and lead it back, without abolishing it, to the super-essential Good, to the Ocean of Beauty, to the One beyond everything.[73]

---

70 Ibid.
71 Ibid., 189.
72 Ibid., 189, n. 25.
73 Ibid., 191.

SIX

The Sense of Reality

The link between the sense of the supernatural and the sense of being must first be made clear and this will be done, as a brief introduction, in the first section, drawn from Borella's The Sense of the Supernatural.

Next, we recall that during the myth of the cave (see Chapter 5 above) it was stated that "the sense of the reality is one with intelligence." This clearly deserves several comments. Thus, a second section, drawing from Borella's Penser l'analogie, *will provide a first insight into this ontological experience before the third and fourth sections, drawn from* The Crisis of Religious Symbolism, *will bring us back to first principles and their connaturality with intelligence.*

Additionally, we will argue that, if the intellect is the perception of being, the will is basically the desire for being. This is the subject of the fifth section, drawn from Amour et vérité.

Finally, the 'The Paradox of Epimenides' (cf. The Crisis of Religious Symbolism, *Chapter 9) has given Jean Borella the opportunity to bring together intelligence, will and reason in order to understand how they combine with each other yet remain distinct. This will be addressed in our sixth section.*

Sense of the Supernatural and Sense of Being

If religious agnosticism and the relativism of knowledge are inseparable, this is because, for modernism, there is no speculative statement that can carry any ontological significance, or any religious speculative statement that is able to have an objective meaning for relative and historic man.[1] "Once one denies the sense of the supernatural (or denies the possibility of believing that a supernatural reality can exist), one also denies the ontological value of cognitive statements, for

---

1 *The Sense of the Supernatural* (Edinburgh: T & T Clark, 1998), 38.

these two things are interdependent. Or, if one prefers, ontology and theology are intertwined."[2] Indeed, if human knowledge can go out of itself and focus on an objective being it "in some way finds its complete and more-than-perfect model in the act of faith by which Being as such, coming from without and revealing itself, is welcomed into the intellect. Far from being opposed to intellectual knowledge, revelation provides it with an unsurpassable and fulfilling norm. Faith is the truth of knowledge. All human knowledge aspires to this revelation which is realized by faith and by means of which Reality itself is made known to the intellect — yet without attaining it. What poet, what scholar, what philosopher has not dreamed of a knowledge that would be the very being of things, the *logos*, the revealing word that would speak directly to him?"[3]

This is why the power that our intelligence has to perceive being conditions the possibility of dogmatic statements. "The Divine Sun can indeed reveal itself to blind eyes, provided they are first healed of their blindness, but It would in no way reveal Itself to sightless beings. Thus . . . the loss of the sense of the supernatural is but the religious aspect of the loss of the sense of the ontological, or the intuition of being, and vice versa."[4]

The Intuition of Being

This innate intuition of the meaning of being seems to be the 'memory' of our ontological origin. When the creature is endowed with intelligence, it cannot but carry within the substance of its mind the memory of this 'ontological event' when Being endowed it with being. This is the testimony of our 'awareness of intelligibility', our 'semantic experience'. This is the only method available to us in metaphysics, a method that finds that the idea of being, in its semantic reverberations in our intelligence, cannot be explained by any genesis and is therefore innate.[5]

Thus, we can define intelligence as a sense of being or of the real. This idea appears therefore to be primary and ultimately identified with the idea of First Being.[6] This idea of First Being — only culture and reflection enable us

2   Ibid., 37–8.
3   Ibid., 38.
4   Ibid.
5   *Penser l'analogie*, III.
6   Ibid., III–12.

to become aware of It — is what remains of the super-conscious experience of God at the timeless moment of our creation. In this sense, it is an immediate experience of God at the heart of our being, which is part of what is true in *ontologism* — its mistake was to argue that we have direct access to this immediate experience of First Being.[7]

It is precisely the immediacy of this ontological experience that makes it inaccessible to us in a direct way, just as we cannot, except indirectly, see the light by which we see. This is why we can only indirectly grasp the Being Who causes us to be by accepting the gift of being given us and thus fulfilling His creative will.

The Intuition of the Real

By knowing itself, the intellect knows first principles implicitly: "They are, however, posited and defined as such only by the intellect reflecting on its own cognitive activity, when it becomes aware of the natural structures brought into play by this activity. Knowledge of them therefore implies an initial intellectual act . . . [which is] essentially an intuition of the real as such . . . an awareness that something is real (or again: being is meaningful for the intellect)."[8]

Saint Thomas Aquinas expresses it as follows: "Our intellect, therefore, knows being naturally, and whatever essentially belongs to being as such; and upon this knowledge is founded the knowledge of first principles, such as the impossibility of simultaneously affirming and denying, and the like. Thus only these principles are known naturally by the intellect."[9] And also: "Our intellect knows some things naturally; thus the first principles of the intelligibles, whose intelligible conceptions . . . exist naturally in the intellect and proceed from it."[10]

The Intellect and the Sense of the Real

"We give the name of intelligence or intellect to what in us knows." On the side of the known object, "what is received in the intellect is not its own being

---

7 Ibid.

8 *The Crisis of Religious Symbolism*, 316.

9 *Contra Gentiles*, II, 83, 8; cf. *The Crisis of Religious Symbolism*, 317.

10 *Contra Gentiles*, IV, 11. We need to recognize that for St. Thomas, there is a knowledge that does not come from the senses, for instance when he states that "certain seeds of knowledge pre-exist in us" (*De veritate*, XI, I, *ad. Resp.*); cf. *The Crisis of Religious Symbolism*, 316.

but the intelligible modality of its own being, stripped of its own individual existence. . . . The act of knowledge is therefore realized only at the price of a kind of derealization."

"And yet knowledge is indeed real, even a preeminent function of the real. There is being only for knowledge. . . . Just as *sugared* or *salted* is only meaningful to the tongue, just as *visible* and *audible* are only meaningful to the eye and ear, so the 'real' is only meaningful to the intellect — and therefore the intellect is the faculty for distinguishing real from unreal."

This situation of the intellect is paradoxical: it is at once outside of and bound up with the real, a situation where "the light illuminating it comes from elsewhere . . . is of a different nature and of a different level of reality than the level on which it is manifested. . . . The cognitive content of the intellect exceeds the degree of reality of its manifestation; in other words, it is transcendent to it."[11]

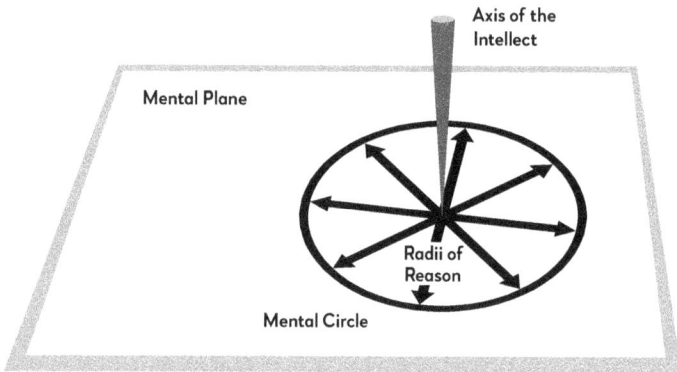

Intellect and Will: the Two Modes of the Spirit

Knowledge, as an intelligible communion of the knower and the known, but at a distance, as an anticipated fusion of subject and object, is this very anticipation to the extent that this fusion is incomplete.[12] Conversely, this anticipation reveals a desire for this fusion. And this desire is the will. "The intellect is 'sense of being' and only speaks of being. But it is vision only on condition of not being what it sees, which is however reality itself. This is why

11 *Amour et vérité*, iii–12.
12 Ibid., 117.

desire for this reality, born of a 'vision' of being, is yet found to be necessarily 'blind'. Since to see being is to hold it at a distance, this vision, which withdraws us from being at the very instant that it is given to us, must be renounced if we are willing to attain that which is communicated to us by desire. There must be an obscure side to a mirror; otherwise there is no reflection. Likewise there is an obscure side to the intellect, and this is the will, which is basically the desire for being, just as intellect is a perception of being. The will then seems to be another mode of the spirit."[13]

However, these two opposing modes — intellect and will — are inseparable and complementary. They are the poles of the spirit: a cognitive and an ontological pole. And if the will possesses something of the unintelligible, this is because it is this "force that rises from the depths of one's being" and therefore something that the intellect cannot grasp: this being is the proper self just this side of the intellect, "the backing of the mirror thanks to which the mirror is not simply transparent."[14]

This complementarity of intellect and will is illustrated by the parable of the Blind Man and the Paralytic: the intellect is powerless without the will; the will without the intellect is blind. However, as intelligence is the spirit which realizes the unity of the human being (since it includes all other modalities), we can see that it "is itself a mode of being and will a mode of knowledge" (consider, for example, the amazing intelligence evident in biological functions such as cardiac rhythm, respiration, etc.).

And if there is one place where intellect and will are in equilibrium — tending towards the spirit which is their unity — this is love: to love is "to desire what the intelligence makes known to us as good. . . . In love the ego discovers it is not the true center of being, since this center seems at once, in the will's impulse, to be more profound than it, and, in the intellect's attraction, loftier than it."[15]

Intelligence requires the Grace of Faith

Even though there is no essential heterogeneity between our intelligence and the *Logos*, this does not mean that the intellect works only with identities.

13 Ibid.
14 Ibid.
15 Ibid., 118.

To the contrary, the intellect is fundamentally searching for unlikeness, dissimilarity, otherness.

Indeed, intelligence reveals the intelligible nature of everything it touches because it opens itself to the otherness of its object: in itself, being is as it were an essential otherness. This is intelligence as the sense of the real, sense of being. Intelligence "fulfills its own nature only in its openness and submission to something other than itself, it receives its completion only as it becomes present to something else, its own 'other side' first and foremost. . . . This is true for sensible as well as metaphysical knowledge."[16]

This paradox of intelligence is illustrated by the scholastic adage: "nothing is in the intellect that was not first in the senses"; and by its correction by Leibniz: "except for the intellect itself."[17] For it is by submitting to its objective other, being, this 'beyond' to which it is ordered, that the intelligence rediscovers itself precisely in the sense of a Platonic reminiscence.

To be invested with being, all the intellect has to do is consent to be open to the object of its aspirations, just as the eye opens and turns to see what it needs to see. This dark side of the intellective mirror (without which it would not be a mirror), this dependency of the intellect that is an existential putting-down of roots, is the will. There is no intellection that does not require, at its root, the acquiescence of the will. However, for the will (blind by definition) to acquiesce to the openness of intellect, it must be capable of some cognitive perception, and this intelligence of the will corresponds to the will of the intelligence.[18]

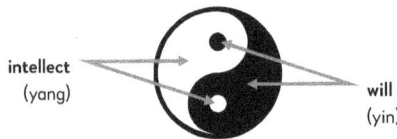

intellect (yang) → will (yin)

To avoid this endless regression — the intellect supposing the will which supposes the intellect — we simply have to remember that these "are not

---

16 *The Crisis of Religious Symbolism*, 318.

17 Leibniz, *New Essays on Human Understanding,* II, ch. I, §2, III (trans. Remnant & Bennett [Cambridge: Cambridge University Press, 1996]); *The Crisis of Religious Symbolism*, 318.

18 In the representation of the intellect and will according to the Far Eastern yin-yang symbol, we can say that the will is yin and includes a luminous point and that intellect is yang and has a dark side. Cf. *The Crisis of Religious Symbolism*, 319, note 1.

two distinct 'things' but two modes of being of the same spiritual entity: the person." Furthermore, we can say that this agreement between intellect and will, "humanly inexplicable — but not impossible — is precisely the work of grace. This intervention from 'On High' is required to incite the will, on the one hand to allow the intellect to be open to the light, and on the other to be itself obedient to the reality perceived by the intellect."[19]

The multiple forms of this grace are:

- Faith — and every intellection requires the grace of this faith.
- But also a revelation, a culture, an education to train the will and teach it how to comply with the perception of truth.

Thus we need to distinguish in intelligence:

¶ The autonomy of its pure act: we cannot learn to understand or control the intellective grasp. This is what Simone Weil has shown. "The intellect, in its act of intellection, is perfectly free, and no authority, no will, even our own, has any power over it: one cannot be forced to understand what is not understood."[20]

¶ The fact that potential intelligence — that is, intelligence when it is not in act — is educable. This education of intelligence, as far as its active structuring is concerned, is reason: an acquired submission of the mind to norms.

Reason "is identical to rationality's will, to that *willed* part of intellect that, without any real intuition of the truth, swears an oath to conduct itself according to its principles, perceived as demands. . . . But this oath can be broken, precisely because it depends, in its very being, on an implicit and almost unconscious act of the will."[21]

If the will exhausts itself in obeying what somehow completely eludes it, this is folly or madness: a breaking of the pact that binds us to the *Logos*, a discovery that it is only a pact or, at any rate, no longer appears to be such.

19 Ibid.
20 Ibid.
21 Ibid.

To the contrary, the intelligence at the heart of reason encounters the evidence of principles. Its submission is due to its investment with being, but the more submissive it is, the more it is free to fulfill its true nature: "The intellect requires what is intelligible, it is nourished by meaning and lives only for this; in short, the law that constitutes and defines it in its very essence is the *semantic principle.*"[22]

SEVEN

Beyond Being

Is first philosophy ontology (or general metaphysics) or theology (or special metaphysics)? In other words: is being as such being in general or God (First Being)? Much ink has been spilled on this subject.

What is involved here, after briefly reviewing the point of view limited to being as such—a point of view frequently giving rise to difficulties—is rather to 'go' directly beyond being, according to Plato's ground-breaking formula: "the Good is not of the order of the being (ousia), but something beyond being (epekeina tes ousias)."[1] *How is such a thought of Beyond Being possible? We will in fact even see that it is simply unavoidable and that everything leads us to it: logic, the being-knowledge dialectic, analogy . . .*

My aim is therefore to bring together these various 'leaps' of thought as recalled and powerfully formulated by Jean Borella. To begin with, a first article will show that compatibility between being and knowledge requires a supra-ontological place where the metaphysics of being becomes a metaphysics of knowledge:[2] Beyond Being, the dialectical path of being-knowledge. Then a second article, drawing from The Crisis of Religious Symbolism, *will show how logic imposes a metalogic: Beyond Being, the logical way. A third article, drawing from* Penser l'analogie, *will show how analogy is necessarily derived from the first analogy between Being and the Beyond of its affirmation or, in theological language, that first analogy between God and the super-essential Godhead. We will get to this point through the ontology and meontology of the Burning Bush, passing through the possibility of possibility to infinite Possibility to conclude with the realizing[3] distinction between essence and existence in the creature: Beyond Being, the analogical path. Finally, we will see that this very*

---

1 Plato, *Republic*, 509b.
2 See *Problémes de gnose*, 160–211.
3 See below, p. 119 and *Problèmes de gnose*, 170–71.

analogy, through its anagogical power, will surely lead us to this very same supreme Analogy, but this time through the Identity-Otherness paradox that characterizes it: Beyond Being, the way of the Identity-Otherness paradox (see Penser l'analogie).

But first, by way of preface, we have this short extract from The Crisis of Religious Symbolism *to offer as a foretaste:*

"AT THE RELATIVE LEVEL, 'THAT *IS*' MEANS 'THAT IS *possible*', because we know the possibility of a thing, its intelligible nature, its 'logic', its non-contradiction, only from its reality. But, at the level of the Absolute, 'that is possible' means 'that is' (without specifying the mode of being), for, *in divinis*, all that is possible is real (but everything possible is not 'realized' in the relative . . . there are more things in God than can be contained in heaven and earth)."

This is why "the viewpoint of the possible, and therefore of knowledge, surpasses that of being." Saying that the possible is non-contradictory can be interpreted from an ontological and a superontological point of view:

• Ontologically speaking, "it is impossible for a thing to be and not to be. Being is, non-being is not."
• Superontologically speaking, "Absolute possibility is absolute Non-contradiction, that is to say, the Non-contradiction of a Reality that cannot be contradicted by anything, or again to which nothing can be opposed, and therefore which includes in Itself Its own contradiction, or again which eludes every opposition because It eludes every *position* and, first of all, the initial one, the ontological position or affirmation."[4]

Beyond Being: the Dialectical Path of Being-knowledge

Metaphysics, an inherently sacred science, transcends all formulations ascribed to it and all the human receptacles that receive it. "It is precisely the divine Word itself as the 'light that enlightens every man that comes into this world,'

---

4 *The Crisis of Religious Symbolism*, 94–5, note 2.

that is to say, every being that has access to the human condition."[5] It is Guénon's doctrine which, in modern times, not only has restored metaphysical knowledge to its own order but, in addition, might be "characterized in itself as an effective awareness of the real, in such a way that only what we have become effectively aware of is real for us. Everything else can only be defined as possible. Knowledge is thus a 'making real', not in the idealist sense where it would create the real, but in the sense that by it alone is there any reality for mankind. The real is strictly correlative to the act by which one becomes aware of it. . . . "

"[However,] any assertion about the absolutely and infinitely Real seems to sin by both excess and deficiency: by excess, because a relative being is asserting more than it is entitled to say; by deficiency, since this Absolute is no more than an affirmation."[6] To this second difficulty, Guénon answers — characteristically — that it is not the human intellect which affirms the divine Absolute, but the Absolute itself that affirms Itself in each intellect: the *Verbum illuminans*."[7] To the first difficulty (affirmations of the Real being more than we are entitled to), Guénon's original response can be found in *The Multiple States of the Being*:

- First, we must distinguish the Infinite from Universal Possibility, surely for us a virtual distinction (that is to say neither actual nor only from reason — in the scholastic sense), but which is not arbitrary for all that, since it reflects the analogically active and passive 'aspects' of the Supreme.
- The primary benefit of this distinction is that universal Possibility is "the minimum determination required to make . . . the Infinite actually conceivable,"[8] the Infinite which is for us inconceivable in itself. This universal Possibility, a reality limited by nothing, an 'absolute non-contradiction', necessarily encompasses what exceeds Being, and is inevitably counterposed to what is not and what contradicts It. Universal Possibility is thus "barely a determination,

5 "Gnose et gnosticisme chez René Guénon," op. cit., 116–17.
6 Ibid., 117.
7 Ibid.
8 *The Multiple States of the Being*, trans. H. D. Fohr (Ghent, NY: Sophia Perennis, 2001), 11.

a determination which, in truth, only begins with Being. But it would be better to say that Universal Possibility is the universal *determinability* of the Principle which is absolutely undetermined (or super-determined) in Itself."[9]

Beyond Being	The Infinite	Absolute non-determination
	Universal possibility	*Determinability*
Being		Self-determination *sui causa*

- However, the notion of possibility, as distinguished from that of reality, is ambiguous. It signifies whatever can be but is not realized: the essences of creatures 'prior' to any existentiation. In other words, such a definition of possibility serves to reduce it to mere possibilities of manifestation. The possibles only make sense in their realization and we can no longer speak of Supreme Reality as universal Possibility.

- This is why Guénon says that "the distinction between the possible and the real . . . has no metaphysical validity"[10] and that we must distinguish between the possibilities of manifestation (which define all that is manifestable, whether manifested or not) and the possibilities of non-manifestation. But in his chapter "Knowledge and Consciousness," the metaphysical identity of the real and the possible assumes a more specific meaning, these pages containing "in a certain way what the Gospel calls 'the key to gnosis.'"[11]

- More precisely, the word *real* means, for Guénon, that which we have actually assimilated consciously, that which we have 'realized'. However, he extends this proposition much further, not only viewing the realization by knowledge in a new light, by seeing it inseparably as the realization of 'object' as well as 'subject', but claiming that this realization is also based on what might be called a metaphysics of knowledge which, in a sense, replaces a metaphysics of being.[12]

9   "Gnose et gnosticisme chez René Guénon," 118.
10 *The Multiple States of the Being*, 17; cf. *Problèmes de gnose*, 172.
11 *Problèmes de gnose*, 201–5.
12 Ibid.

Let us consider these two points more closely:

1. As for the correlative 'realization' through knowledge, of knowing subject and known object, we can say that there is an actualization of their primary and underlying unity. "The real is correlative to the consciousness we have of the real, and therefore the degree of reality is correlative to the level of consciousness. If, for us, reality is first and immediately the corporeal world, this is because our consciousness is at first purely sensorial, that is, absorbed by the material world. . . . Sensation, says Aristotle, is the common act of the one sensing and the sensible, and the sensible is 'in act' only in sensation. There is no idealism here . . . subject and object are seen from the outset in the unity of their actual relationship."[13] Neither is there any objectivism: the object is not posited as an object which would be an object for no one; nor is there monism. The distinction between subject and object is not denied. The real, in an *actual* sense, is the result of knowledge: the common act of the knower and the known, of the intellect and the intelligible. Conversely, what is not known *at the present time* is not 'real' at *the present time* but must be regarded as possible. "This does not at all mean that whatever we are unaware of at present is entirely non-existent, nor that it would have need of us to gain access to being, but, only strictly speaking, that it is illusory to speak about the reality of something of which we are not actually conscious." This is the illusion "of anyone discussing ontology and unaware of their own existential situation, who, by dint of talking about the only Real, forget that this also needs to be 'realized.'"[14]

Thus, anything that surpasses the level of our present consciousness can be considered as a possibility. This is especially true for whatever is beyond the manifested world, whatever is inaccessible to the actual knowledge of fallen man in his ordinary state. These are those possibilities that man should realize by knowledge,

---

13 Ibid. This is a thesis that "would come rather close to what is most acceptable in Husserl's phenomenology" ("Gnose et gnosticisme chez René Guénon," 120, note 107).

14 "Gnose et gnosticisme chez René Guénon," 120.

and speaking of them as possibilities of non-manifestation avoids a reified ontologism that might result from speaking about the Non-Manifested. In such a case, absolute and infinite Reality would be posited as an object in front of us, denying specifically that It is absolute and infinite. Therefore, It becomes relative to the subject that limits It. Of course, all thought is inevitably objectifying and saving in its own way. It communicates to us the knowledge of the transcendent Object, the Being who created us and Who alone can save us. But are we truly thinking about Non-Being if we think about Being in the same way? It is only as *Universal Possibility* that we can still conceive of the Infinite: "It is not only what in *itself* may be all reality, it is also, and inseparably, what *for us* is universally possible. . . . We cannot separate what is [in Universal Possibility] the unlimited conceptual opening of the thinking subject and what is the infinite Objectivity under the effect of which our intelligence is opened."[15]

2. Let us return now to this metaphysical identity of the possible and the real to show how a metaphysics of knowledge replaces a metaphysics of being. To be able to talk about the identity of the Possible and the Real, we must necessarily "admit that knowledge is absolutely total, or, more accurately, that it has always been so, that is to say, that it is realized in its permanent actuality. This is the only way to speak legitimately at the present time about That which exceeds our individual consciousness, because It is the totalization of all possible knowledge." However, it is not enough to consider the 'realization', completed for all eternity, of total knowledge (which would enable us to speak about this); we must also take into account the possibility of this very act of knowledge. If everything is already accomplished, why do accomplishments still occur? Plato poses the same question: "If knowing is to be acting on something, it follows that what is known must be acted upon by it, and so, on this showing, reality when it is being known by the act of knowledge must, in so far as it is known, be changed owing to being so acted upon — and that, we say, cannot happen

15 Ibid.

to the changeless."[16] In other words, if being is immutable, how can it be known?

"What does the fact of being known mean for this Being, the fact that an act of knowledge can happen to the One that cannot undergo any change?" Knowledge does not happen to Being 'from without', from some inconceivable 'nowhere'. If it is exterior to It, it does not exist; if it is part of It it cannot happen, since Being is immutable. Such knowledge is an impossibility. Hence, the need to go beyond the Being to account for the act of knowledge, "where the Identity of Self with Self is no longer that of an immutability of nature, but transcends the opposition of change and changeless and contains them in a supereminent way, because it is free from any nature or determinate essence." Knowledge in its principal possibility is then an 'aspect of the Infinite'.[17]

"Such a knowledge is exactly what Catholic tradition calls the 'Immaculate Conception', since it is ultimately the Immaculate Conception (pure of any even essential determination) that the Absolute has of Itself. . . . The knowledge-event is therefore eternal. It *takes place* in the permanent and universal actuality of the Supreme (super-ontological) 'Intellect' or active Perfection, which embraces in itself the innumerable relativities of specific awarenesses, insofar as they are included in Passive Perfection. This is the very self-revelation of God to Himself, the 'hidden treasure' that is God and for the knowledge of which He created the world—because God wants to be known and the numerous intellects that open to His mystery are, in reality, so many countless modes in which He becomes aware of Himself. . . . Every time a starry intelligence is born within divine Knowledge there occurs a gnostic 'event', which is nothing but a possibility of the Infinite Itself whenever the Supreme Thearchy realizes the mystery of its new and eternal birth to Itself, whenever the Father begets His Word, His unique and beloved Son in the unity of his Spirit."[18]

16 *Sophist*, 248e, trans. F. M. Cornford, in *Plato, the Collected Dialogues* (Princeton, NJ: Princeton University Press, 1961), 993; cf. "Gnose et gnosticisme chez René Guénon," 121, note 108.
17 René Guénon, *The Multiple States of the Being*, 11; "Gnose et gnosticisme chez René Guénon," 121.
18 "Gnose et gnosticisme chez René Guénon," 116–22.

Beyond Being: the Logical Way

"It is the same to think and the thought that [the object of thought] exists, for without Being, in what has been expressed, you will not find thought,"[19] Parmenides tells us. This is Parmenidean logic: to say something other than being is to say non-being, which is nothing, and therefore this is to say nothing. This is where a strict application of the non-contradiction principle leads, and this is how it reduces the real to what logic can measure! For experiences of error, just like *sophistical* illusions, are 'realities' that speak of what is not while speaking of what is. Parmenidean logic is therefore violence to being, but also to logic: the principle of non-contradiction is contradicted in its very definition. Intelligence, faithful to its own nature, cannot accept this: it notices error and illusion it must account for, and find how this non-reality, or apparent reality, can be integrated into a universal reality. Because intelligence is submission to the real and the sense of the real, intellection is a semantic act. And this semantic principle is ultimately what logic calls the principle of non-contradiction. This is an essential principle, even for its modern critics (such as Lupasco), who claim to develop a 'non-Aristotelian' logic under the pretext that the physically real would present us with some cases of realized contradiction. For it is still in the name of non-contradiction (or concern for rigor) that they want to 'surpass' this principle, which is contradictory.

To speak of what is not is to make non-being be, which seems to violate the principle of non-contradiction. However, "we can actually speak of what is not. This is then because, in a certain manner, non-being does not exclude being: otherwise, this possibility would be unintelligible, extra-semantic. The possibility of stating the principle of non-contradiction implies the reality of non-being."[20]

It is therefore important not to restrict being, which *seems* limited by a principle, but "to the contrary, under the very demands of reality, consider the principle in its most absolute universality, and such that Non-Being itself can no longer contradict Being, that is, accede to a conception of the

19 Fragment VIII, 34–6; in *Parmenides*, trans. L. Tarán (Princeton, NJ: Princeton University Press, 1965), 86; cf. *The Crisis of Religious Symbolism*, 321.
20 *The Crisis of Religious Symbolism*, 322, note 2.

absolute Reality such that It includes in Itself its own contradiction, or again to a conception of a reality non-exclusive to its Otherness, in short a strictly non-contradictory Reality."²¹

We have seen how in the Parmenidean discourse being completely determines the discourse, while in the structuralist discourse it is the discourse that fully determines being. This means that "the semantic principle requires that we surpass the viewpoint of ontological 'determinateness', of being as source and root of all determination, as pure and absolute positivity, as the general formality of all forms. Super-ontological Reality, the absolutely and infinitely Real, is that for which pure Being is itself *only* the symbol, the principial self-determination; it is the metaphysical All-Nothing, the absolutely non-posited, the Beyond of every affirmation (and therefore every negation), the Supreme Non-contradiction, that which can be 'defined' as the infinite Possibility, to the very extent that the Possible is that which comprises no contradiction. By this we clearly see that the logic of being leads us beyond being."²² Being is only the initial 'revelation' of Supreme Reality, the principial self-affirmation. But at the same time, "without this self-affirmation, the *logos* would have no knowledge of Supreme Reality, which is only 'manifested' through it. And besides, neither would there be any *logos*, since this is essentially a sense of being. However, the *logos* would be just as impossible if Supreme Reality, the super-ontological Absolute, were purely and simply identical with its affirmation, in other words if this principial ontological 'manifestation' *exhausted* all of Reality's possibilities. . . . Such is Parmenidean being, the full and solid reality of which excludes every other possibility, that of the super-ontological as well as the infra-ontological. With such a conception being has no 'meaning', nothing can be said about it, since it itself says *nothing*, and therefore the word of being is, precisely, no longer possible."²³

Truly, *logos* can be the *principial utterance* of the sense of being only if being makes sense, and being makes sense only if it is not ultimate Reality, but Its affirmation. It is also the function of the *logos* to be this affirmation, and that is why it is opposed to its negation: "the very negation of being clearly proves that being is an affirmation" (even the first Affirmation). "Thus, in contemplating being, the *logos* is implicitly contemplating the Above-Being, as

21 Ibid., 322.
22 Ibid., 323–24.
23 Ibid., 324.

depthless Depth that 'gives' to the *logos* its meaning under the form of being, that is, under the form of Its ontological self-revelation."

"To 'say' (*logos*) being is to say Above-Being, for, without the Above-Being (or Non-Being) *in which* it is uttered, there would be no *logos*." For the human *logos* facing the Sun of Being, this Sun is the only enlightening experience. If it sets, that is, if the human being turns towards or rather upon himself in imitation of the Earth's rotation, he loses the benefit of this ontological light, but "by the same stroke is revealed then both the sparkling of the super-solar stars and the more-than-luminous Darkness of nocturnal silence that the day-star obliterates with its splendor. This is to say that the creature, in its autonomy and by its own existence, proves, as the hitherside of Being, the super-ontological Reality for which the Sun is itself only the blinding revelation."[24]

The Beyond of Being: the Analogical Path

To simply state that the relation of God to His being is analogous to the relation of the creature to its being is not very enlightening.

- First, because the relationship of God to His being is on the level of identity: God is His very being, which is absolutely not the relationship maintained by the creature with its being — no creature is what it is; it can only, at very most, become such. Is such an analogy of being more than just an identity of words? If, as Gilson says, the respective relations are "infinitely different,"[25] what analogy can be found between God and creature?

- Secondly, because these relations are so radically different that they are heterogeneous. Indeed, the creature is *really* distinct from its being — the essence of a creature being not identical to its existence — and its essence and existence can therefore maintain a real relationship; whereas, in God, essence and existence are identical, which is why we are talking about more than a *relation of reason*. Moreover, when we say "God is his Being," this is only because we grammatically distinguish his Essence from His Being.

24 Ibid., 324–25.

25 Etienne Gilson, *The Spirit of Medieval Philosophy* (London: Sheed & Ward, 1936), 448, note 14; cf. *Penser l'analogie*, 91.

Ontology and Meontology of the Burning Bush. For the idea of a relationship of God with His being to take on real meaning, one needs to get away
from a strict Gilsonian ontology to enter into a (neo-)Platonic metaphysics.
Because the very idea of relationship "requires, for its own possibility, a *fun-
damentum in re* [a basis in the thing itself], lacking this it will remain what it
is in Aristotle an 'accident of an accident', 'the most feeble of all beings.'"[26]

This basis can only be metaphysical; it denotes, within the depths of absolute
Reality, a supreme Relationship within the depths of the identity of the One,
a kind of Otherness. There alone is the ultimate root of relationship. With
reference to this issue of analogy, this supreme Relationship can be seen as the
one that the diving Being maintains with the Divine Essence of the infinite
Godhead, as long as we 'locate' this Essence 'beyond being'. In the words of
Plato: "The Good is not of the order of being (*ousia*), but something beyond
being (*epekeina tes ousias*)."[27]

Pure being, the first that is 'thinkable' (since the thought of anything initially requires the thought of its possibility), appears as the first or principal
determination, beyond which there is the Naught of any determination,
absolute Non-Affirmation. From the side of existing things, of the multiplicity
of creaturely determinations, pure Being appears as their ontological root;
seen from 'the other side', the super-ontological or me-ontological Essence,
pure Being is the first Affirmation, the eternal Self-Affirmation of the Divine
Essence, the Divine Essence insofar as it is able to be designated and named.

According to the order of grace and salvation, God and His Name are
identical; yet according to the requirements of metaphysical discernment,
'Being' is the Name of the Divine Essence, but not the Essence itself in its
radical selfhood. In the *Sum Qui Sum* ('I am who I am') of the Burning Bush,
the first 'I am' refers to the unfathomable and unspeakable Essence and the
second one to the Being-Name, the Determiner of all these 'names' that are the
creatures; while the 'Who', linking the One to the Other, is the basis for the
eternal and principial Relationship that the Divine Being maintains with the
Divine Essence, a Relationship that is the Source of all created relationships.[28]
Thus, "Being is the first Analogue of the super-essential Godhead. If there is

26 *Penser l'analogie*, 92.
27 Plato, *Republic*, 509b; cf. *Penser l'analogie*, 92, n. 4.
28 *Penser l'analogie*, 94.

truly an analogy of being, this is because Being is preeminently the first Analogy, from which all others are derived and upon which all others depend."[29]

Being and beings are no more contradictory than Being and Non-Being. This is also why, if we designate the God-Name by Being and the super-essential Essence by Non-Being, there is no contradiction, despite Heidegger and the reproach of onto-theology:

- for Being is the only access to the mystery of God, Who in the Burning Bush calls Himself "Being is my name." Therefore, without ontology, no theology.
- Conversely, "without theology, no real ontology. Only the identification of being with the preeminent Being that is God removes it from the abstractness of a concept and situates it in the mystery of its living transcendence."[30]

For the full validity of the principle of non-contradiction (A cannot be both A and non-A, or non-A and A are mutually exclusive and cannot be true at the same time), within its parameters of the ontology of substance, there is substituted in the meontological (or meta- or super-ontological) order the principle of absolute non-contradiction. In fact, by adherence to an ontology of substance, the Divine Being is at risk of being numbered among created beings. The difficulty is that philosophical thought "cannot account for the being of contingent realities without invoking the need for the reality of a necessary and first Being and that, at the same time, these two kinds of being are contraposed to each other. Thus, with respect to this necessary Being, which nevertheless endows them with being, contingent beings are as if they were not."[31]

To glimpse how it would be possible that Divine Reality is not opposed to the contingent reality of the creature, we should above all not do away with a God-Being (since the need for a First Being is well-established), but go beyond a strictly ontological point of view, so as to, without eliminating Being, enable us to imagine the metaphysical condition of its possibility.

29 Ibid., 95.
30 Ibid., 96.
31 Ibid., 98.

Possibility, contingency and the possibility of possibility. Where defined as "what may *or* may not be," possibility is limited to one aspect of the possible, that of its non-necessity, which reduces possibility to contingency. However, possibility is, above all, a non-impossibility; that is, before anything can be *or* not be, it is necessary that it can be, that it is not impossible. Therefore, possibility being what may be, it should be viewed in two different ways:

- The possibility of self-realization (the knife can cut), which is a relative, extrinsic possibility in that it refers to the ability of the subject.
- The possibility of this possibility or absolute possibility, intrinsic to the compatibility of the constituent parts of the subject's nature (the knife is possible, given a solid and able-to-be-finely *sharpened* material, which excludes gas or wood). This absolute possibility is, of course, the possibility of the essence; whether it exists or not in nature, the circle is possible, while a circle-square or 'gaseous vertebrate' (Ruyer) is contradictory and thus impossible.

Thus, a thing is possible as long as it is not contradictory, even if it does not exist in the world of cosmic realities. This means that it is real in the metaphysical order; "it is even an eternal and necessary reality." In other words, in the divine order, all that is possible is necessarily true: everything that can be *is*, or else the Divine Being would not be all essence and would be limited. There are therefore some possibles that will never come into existence: the 'non-beings' (*non-entia*). Because God is an infinite possibility necessarily overflowing all creation, created creation could not exhaust the creatable in God.

These non-beings are therefore purely intrinsic possibles, perfect examples "of those essences that we are entitled to consider in themselves without any ordination to the creation . . . [and] this is rightly how it is with divine transcendence: If the immeasurable overwhelms the created, this is strictly a consequence of the infinite creative Essence."[32]

If these possibilities are indeed pure, how are they still possible? In relation to their conceivability by the Divine Intellect!

What is possible is what is non-contradictory, and the non-contradictory is the conceivable. However, it is not *our* conceivable that defines the possible

---

32 Ibid., 102.

any more than it is something's actually verified existence. "Only the divine Intelligence 'measures' possibility; it is because the possibles are eternally conceived in the Divine Word that they are possibly conceivable for our intelligence, our intelligence which is a participation with the *Logos*."[33]

Infinite possibility. What remains is that the possibility of being — the essence of which is not composed of elements capable (or not) of being intrinsically compatible — does not involve an intrinsic non-contradiction. Clearly, we must therefore oppose being to what is not: to nothingness — each being, "in a certain manner, the condition for the possibility of the other." Thus, "in the order of thought, being only makes sense in its difference from nothingness, while, in the order of reality, nothingness only makes sense thanks to its relationship to the being it denies."[34] On the basis of this analogical unity of being — which affords a certain unity of meaning, regardless of the being to which it is applied, even in the case of First Being — we must also speak of possibility for First Being. But, of course, there is a distinction:

- as to its meaning, the possibility of second or existential being (the creature) refers us back to the idea of nothingness from which the *esse* springs forth, that is to say, to something that can only be thought;
- as for First Being, the Supreme Possibility must be regarded as a metaphysical Reality, *the* Supreme Reality, the meontological Principe; "in other words Non-Being, out of which the existential fact springs forth, will have nothingness be, as it were, Its inverted, ultimate and elusive reflection."[35]

The notions of First Being, of First Affirmation and First Positivity only make sense in relation to the unsituatable 'background' out of which they detach themselves. "We cannot think about this meontological background in Itself. We can only think about it in relation to Being, as that which is the basis of its Possibility." So, just as what is possible is what is non-contradictory and the non-contradictory is what is conceivable, "absolute Possibility is the absolute Non-Contradiction and therefore the absolute conceivability. . . . We

---

33 Ibid., 104.
34 Ibid., 104–5.
35 Ibid., 106.

can say then that infinite Possibility is the *Immaculate Conception* in which the meontological essence of the Godhead is conceived of as 'I am'; or even as the fathomless Deep, boundless Space in which Being is conceived in an 'immaculate' manner; that is, without this Conceived, the ontological Point, the principial Self-Determination (or Self-Affirmation), is a 'stain' (*macula*), a 'mark' that would darken, would contradict the pure transparency of the Divine Matrix." [36]

The realizing *distinction of essence and existence in creatures.* What can the doctrine of infinite Possibility bring to this initial question of the analogy between the relation that the Essence of God and the creature each maintain with their respective beings when we have seen that God is with His being in a relation of identity while the creature with its being is in a relation of distinction?

We have said that in God there was no *real* distinction (but only one of reason) between His Essence and His Existence. But what about the creature? Must we subscribe to the *Thomistic* point of view of a "real distinction between essence and existence," when this expression is not found explicitly in St. Thomas?

Now, whatever the issues we can agree on, the fact is that "no creature is truly *what* it is (its essence, its nature), but, to be, it has to realize this essence. Thus the distinction or distance between existence and essence is not so much real as *realizing*. . . . For to ex-ist (*ex-sistere*) is to stand (*sistere*) outside of (*ex*) oneself, outside one's real locus. This is the distance of a created 'existing' from its own essence which defines 'creatureliness' as such." [37] And in this tension between existence and essence we find both the duty to realize our nature (becoming what we are) and the risk of not succeeding; in other words, here lies the possibility of original sin and human freedom.

This creaturely distance between essence and existence can then be related to the principial and non-oppositional distinction of the infinite Essence and Its ontological Determination. And this distance "appears as the trace of the meontological root of Being that the Creator has left on His work. In other words, because there is something of the 'More than Being', there is a 'lesser being' that is the existing being. In the light of this viewpoint, the analogy of

36 Ibid., 108.
37 Ibid., 114–15.

proportionality finds its real (and not only logical) meaning and a real basis that it also helps to reveal: the relative indeterminacy of created existence with respect to its essence is the inverted reflection, the inverse analogy, of the principial non- (or super-) determination of the Divine Essence with respect to Its Being."[38]

"Created substance exercises its own act of being only through its dependence on the communication of the Act of the divine being. Such is, with St. Thomas, the basis for the transcendental analogy of being. The analogical unity of the multiple meanings of being is assured by a participatory communication of the Act of the divine being, thus avoiding the insignificance of equivocality."[39]

Beyond Being: the Way of the Identity-Otherness Paradox

If we say that painted fruit is analogous to natural fruit or that the grape is to the grapevine what the apple is to the apple tree, there is a repeated assertion of a relationship but not an actual understanding of the relationship itself. Such relationships are all effects, never the cause; we are chasing shadows that merge with and separate from each other. To the contrary, these effects, if recognized as such, can teach us that they are analogous to their cause. If we obey its bidding to be recognized as such, the true meaning of analogy will be revealed. No analogy should be horizontal; being the fulfillment of meaning, analogy is itself fulfilled in the *logos* and leads to it. Since the *Logos* is repeated in the sensible world as in a mirror, we can define analogy as the reverberation of the cosmic *Logos*; and it is the vertical dimension that symbolically accounts for this analogy. But let us not then forget that analogies are of two kinds, namely direct analogy and inverse analogy, if the reflection in the sensible world is the inverse of its model, like the reflection of a tree in water. The first one reveals the nature of things, the second their true hierarchy.

According to direct analogy, we see the plant prevail over the mineral, the animal over the plant, and man over all, life being more than the inert and intelligence more than life. All the world's natures 'are' intelligible realities,

---

38   Ibid., 115.

39   Ibid., 117. In what follows Borella shows how this doctrine also obviates the risk of uniqueness. Cf. *Penser l'analogie*, 118–32.

but the loftier they are, the more we risk taking the image for the model. This is where inverse analogy comes in: it bears witness that 'they are not', these intelligible realities are that for which they are analogies. For example, the mineral, barely a part of the sensible world, is best at eluding corruption and change, recreating the innermost face of the changeless essences, while man, the noblest of creatures, can just as well be the most corrupt.

And analogy forces us to go higher still, because the essences themselves could not be their own analogies, their own inversion. In this way we discover that the necessary inversion of the analogical relationship is nothing but the principle of Otherness at the source of the cosmic reverberation of the *Logos*. For, if the analogy is the repetition of Identity, is not Otherness the first inversion of Identity? And this reversal, this Otherness, is at work within the Supreme Identity itself, because it is not so much the inversion of this Identity as the inversion of its affirmation. Its direct analogue is the affirmation of identity, made necessary to the very extent that Identity implies its analogy of itself by itself. This affirmation of identity posited as Identity would be equivalent to a going outside of itself, if it were not made possible and negated at the same time by Otherness, the inverse analogy of Identity. There is nothing outside of Identity; therefore there is nothing there. This is why Otherness, which establishes and denounces the illusory exteriority of principial Affirmation, leads back and reabsorbs this affirmation into sheer Identity by its very otherness; because Otherness, in its super-intelligible essence, is always other than itself. The Other is Other, and is none other than the Same. It is the permanent inversion of its inversion, the absolute negation of its absolute negation. Thus, only the Supreme Identity which is beyond the essences, beyond Being and Non-Being, is in itself its own analogue; It is sheer analogy. In the mystery of Supreme Analogy lies the mystery of the creation of the world: the sensible world, by all the non-being with which it is mixed, bears witness to the still-illusory nature of the intelligible world of which it is a direct reflection, and leads back to the super-intelligible.[40]

40 Ibid., 210–14. This excerpt comes from the final two rejoinders of Socrates in a dialogue on analogy with the mathematician Thales and the painter Zeuxis.

EIGHT

Metaphysic of Christian Mystery

*If this presentation of Jean Borella's work ends on a high note with this intro-
duction to a metaphysic of the Christian mystery,[1] this is because theoretical
metaphysics is, by itself, inoperative. It can become operative "only on the
condition of grafting its (abstract) universality onto the singularity of a new
tree of life planted by God* [a new Revelation] *in the soil of our existence."[2]
For "the concept of religion cannot save any more than the concept of fire can
burn. And the beauty or glamour of formulas that make a concept look good
changes nothing."[3]*

Thus, a first article will show how creation demands both hands of God
(cf. Amour et vérité*) and why Christ should not belong to that category of
Hinduism called 'avatara' (cf.* Christ the Original Mystery*).*

*A second article will then show how the vertical Identity of Christ-Word-Son
is the essential Relationship, at each microcosmic, macrocosmic and metacosmic
'level' (cf.* Amour et vérité*).*

*Finally, a third section will show how Marian theology can lead to a meta-
physical understanding of both the cosmic order and the divine order itself.*

Christ and the Holy Spirit, the two Hands of God in Creation

"All things were created by the *Logos* who is as it were a divine nexus, the
threshold from which flow the creative outpourings, the particular *logoi* of
creatures, and the center towards which in their turn all created beings tend,

---

1 This material was presented in Bruno Bérard, *Introduction à une métaphysique des
mystères chrétiens* (Paris: l'Harmattan, 2005). This version rectifies a few imperfections.

2 Jean Borella, "Intelligence spirituelle et surnaturel," op. cit., 28.

3 Ibid.

as to their final end."[4] But, even if the Word contains the exemplary causes of all things, this is not properly creative power, but it is *through* it that the creative power of the Father transits. And where is the world created? *In the Holy Spirit*: "the Father has created everything through the Son in the Holy Spirit, for wherever the Word is there is the Spirit, and what the Father produces receives its existence through the Word in the Holy Spirit."[5] "In the creative act it is necessary to understand the Father as 'principial' cause of all that is made, the Son as 'demiurgic' cause, the Spirit as 'perfecting' cause. . . . There is only one sole principle of beings, which creates through the Son and perfects in the Spirit."[6]

The work of creation requires the participation of the 'two hands of God': the Word and the Holy Spirit.[7] If a sensible reality can symbolize an intelligible reality this is by virtue of an ontological correspondence, the work of the divine Word. But what brings sensible and intelligible realities into correspondence, what brings the symbolizing towards the symbolized, that is to say the symbol itself, is the work of the Holy Spirit.

Facing the Form of Forms (the Word) and the *procession* of Intelligence (given by the Trinitarian Son) there is therefore this mysterious *materia prima*. This mystery, called *Maya* in India, appears here as a mystery of Love and cosmic Charity. This Charity is the place, the receptacle, the matrix in which God can establish Creation. God casts before Himself his Divine Charity and the created exteriority into which He brings forth His creatures. But because this exteriority is charity and love of God, it brings everything back to Him, this exteriority being nothing but the mode in which God comes towards Himself out of His own Beyond. Charity alone can account for the inconceivable otherness that is creation with respect to the Creator.

The Holy Spirit is therefore this cosmic Charity in which God creates the world; and God could not create in anything other than the Holy Spirit because the Spirit is hypostatic Charity. The Father gives being — being is a gift and Gift is the name of the Holy Spirit. It is He who conveys being from the Principle to creatures and, at the same time, brings the creatures back to

---

4 Vladimir Lossky, *The Mystical Theology of the Eastern Church* (Crestwood, NY: St. Vladimir's Seminary Press, 1976), 99; quoted in Borella, *Amour et vérité*, 307–8.

5 St. Athanasius, *Epistola III ad Serapionem*, § 5, *P.G.*, t. XXVI, col. 632b–c.

6 St. Basil of Caesarea, *Treatise on the Holy Spirit*, 136b.

7 *Contra Haereses* IV, praefatio, *P.G.*, t. VII, col. 975b.

their Principle. He is the universal lodestone that holds together all created beings, balancing the effects of the creative centrifugal force exerted towards the periphery of the *Rota Mundi*, the cosmic Wheel, with the attractive force of Love which turns the circumference to its uncreated Center. Divine immanence is no longer to be sought for . . .

Creation is terrible for the creatures that it distances from their Principle, but, simultaneously, it is "a permanent return from exteriority towards the interiority of the One, since the Holy Spirit gathers up this cosmic scattering by encompassing everything within the arms of His eternal Love."[8]

Consequently, strictly speaking Christ is not an *avatara* according to Hindu terminology, and cannot be reduced to this category. An *avatara* is, in fact, a 'descent' of God, or a 'manifestation' of the divine nature that can assume the nature of non-personal beings, such as fish, wild boar or rocks, which will make obvious in the visible world the presence of the divine and signify, with the help of cosmic forms, its power, greatness, royalty, etc.

Although the Incarnation of Christ does not exclude this general theophanic aspect, it is essentially radically different. Indeed, in Christianity, it is not God as such who was made flesh, but the Word, the Second Person of the Trinity. And "[w]hat matters here is not the *nature,* but the *hypostasis.* It is not Divine Nature that assumes human nature, it is the Hypostasis of the Son, and this metaphysical difference brings with it decisive consequences in the respective economies of each of the religions,"[9] that is of Christianity and Hinduism.

Christ came in the flesh assuming human nature, together with his divine nature, as the Person of the only Son. This redeeming assumption of our whole human nature — this is the mystery of the hypostatic union (two natures, one person). This accomplishment (the Passion and Crucifixion), when seen from without, is the trite story of a religious agitator. But its infinite redemptive value comes "from the single fact that it was lived and 'sustained in being', *invisibly,* by the very Person of the Son. . . . Only faith, and theological faith, discerns, behind the anecdotal and the factual, the hypostatic Principle."[10]

---

8 *Amour et vérité*, 298–99 and 306.
9 *Christ the Original Mystery*, 454.
10 Ibid., 455.

Christ, the Word and Son, the essential Relationship

At each 'level' of this vertical identity Jesus Christ, the Word, and the Son, appears as the essential Relationship or the Essence of Relationship, surely an essence beyond and containing all other essences. Thus, as the Son, He is the prototypical Subsistent Relation within the Trinity; as the Word, He is, cosmologically speaking, the ontological Relationship of the created to the uncreated; as Christ, He is the pre-eminent Relationship, especially inherent to the link that connects man to his neighbor, but also to the one that makes of Christ the neighbor, because any neighbor is always Christ ("It is to me that you did it"!).

The Son is the prototypical Trinitarian Subsistent Relation. "And the Word was with God" (John 1:1): such is the literal translation of the Greek *pros ton theon*, which refers to the *ad intra* relation of the Trinity. Indeed, *pros* means 'turned towards' and 'in relation with', and 'God' (*theon*) preceded by the article 'the' (*ton*) in St. John means 'the Father', whereas in the text that immediately follows ("the Word was God"), *theos* is not preceded by the article and means the Divine Essence. If by the expression "and the Word was with God" John affirms the identity of the Word with the Divine Essence, by "and the Word was *towards **the*** God," he is acknowledging the Son as Relationship with the Father; these two statements, following in succession, express the mystery of the Subsistent Relation within the Trinity, the first of which (both ontologically and logically) is the Son.

The Son is therefore the prototype of any relationship, the prototypical relationship. Anything related to the Subsistent Relation derives from the Son in a certain manner, just as whatever is of the order of the Hypostasis derives from the Holy Spirit. In other words, the Son makes us understand how a person can be a relationship, just as the Holy Spirit, the bond of Love of the Father and the Son, makes us understand how a bond can be a person. And indeed, this is how Latin theology, which considers the Trinity from a relational point of view, sees it from the vantage point of the Son, while Greek theology, which sees it from the hypostatic point of view, sees it from the vantage point of the Holy Spirit.

In any case, the Son, since He is the prototypical subsistent relation, is the metaphysical basis for the relationship of proximity.

The Word is the ontological relation of the created to the uncreated. *By* and *in* are the prepositions of the Word in the liturgy ('by Him and in

Him') and in Scripture. They are also of course in the prologue of St. John's Gospel: *omnia per ipsum facta sunt . . . in ipso vita erat*: "all things have been made *by* Him . . . *in* Him was life" (John 1:3–4); and in St. Paul: "Everything was created *in* Him . . . it is *by* Him that everything was created" (Col. 1:16).

As we have seen, *by* and *in* refer not directly to the creative power (appropriate to the Father) but the creative act. It is the Word through whom creation is produced, the One who connects creation to the Creator because He is the bond between Cause and effect, the ontological relationship in which all beings and all levels of creation subsist, because in Him they are attached to and communicate with the Principle of being.

Together these two prepositions of the Word express the Subsistent ('in') Relation ('by').

Christ is the pre-eminent relation of proximity. If the Trinity is the basis for hypostatized Charity in the Person of the Holy Spirit whose name this is (as in Thomas Aquinas) and who reveals it, the Son, the prototypical Subsistent Relation, establishes the relation of proximity inherent to the neighbor. You will love (love's revealer, the Holy Spirit) thy neighbor (relation of proximity, the Word) as yourself (Person, the Holy Spirit). To love our neighbor is thus to discover that a person is a relation of proximity, just as the Trinitarian mystery identifies the divine Person with a Relationship, and the Son with the prototypical Relationship. This discovery — this act of love — is surely the work of the Holy Spirit, but its result is to reveal the Son who, hypostatically speaking, precedes it.

So love leads to knowledge, the Holy Spirit leads to the Son, just as there is a pneumatization (Holy Spirit) of the intellect (*Logos*) in the alchemy of our inner life. But to this logical foundation we can add a real foundation. This foundation is the Incarnation-Redemption according to which Christ remains present in Person, by His grace, in the act of love. And this foundation is real because it is not the result of a deduction; the Incarnation is a fact, irreducible — this alone should be our starting-point.

And it is indeed fitting that it is the Son who incarnates, because the Incarnation is essentially a work of mediation: Christ is *mediator Dei et hominum*, as the Son is the eternal *medium quo* of the Trinity, the means by which the Divine Essence enters into relation with itself. It is through Christ, the mediator in essence, that men enter mutually into a relation of proximity with themselves and with God. In Jesus Christ we love God, and also in Him does man become the neighbor of God. And it is through the humanity of Christ, the Word-Son, that God can love all men.

To love our neighbor is therefore to put on Christ, to establish oneself in a relationship of proximity or rather let oneself be imbued with the hypostatic relationship, basically dependent on the Incarnation and the continued Incarnation that is the sacraments. Therefore, in order to meet Christ where He is in the neighbor — for our spiritual consciousness is only in potency — we must first meet Him in the sacraments where He is in act. Only under the effect of an actual sacramental presence can the charitable power be actualized, for nothing can move from potency to act except under the effect of a being in act, and only Being is truly in Act.

"*It is to Me that you have done it* (Matthew 25:40, 45): not to the Father or the Spirit, but to the Son, for, by virtue of the hypostatic union, there is only one Self in Christ. . . . The last cause and the first is the Divine Neighbor himself, that hypostatic Proximity which, to unfold its effects in the relative order, utilizes both other people and oneself as created supports for uncreated Proximity. . . . [T]he aim of the act of love is not 'others' as such, but others as neighbor,"[11] and the only neighbor is Christ. In other words, the neighbor "is as it were the matter of proximity, Christ is the eternal Form."[12]

What remains is that, if Christ is the basis for Charity in its sheer necessity, the Holy Spirit, the last Word of the Trinity, is hypostatic Charity itself in its sheer gratuity. And this last Word is co-eternal with the first. In It transpires that realization of the conversion of the Divine Essence back to the Father through the Son.[13]

The Virgin: From Cosmic Order to Divine Order

The Virgin, who is such by the necessarily virginal conception of Christ, is also, even before her birth and in anticipation of Divine Motherhood (Theotokos), *the Immaculate Conception. This creature, apart from any other, is unfailingly the object of a special devotion from the beginning of the Church. And when the need arose, the proclamations of the dogmas of the*

---

11 *Amour et vérité*, 248–49.
12 Ibid., 250.
13 Ibid.

Immaculate Conception and of the Assumption reminded us of her unique and greatly esteemed position.

Now, by the power of symbols attributable to the Theotokos, Marian theology is given a metaphysical interpretation: first, in the cosmic order, where the Virgin symbolizes universal charity and the cosmic matrix; then, in the divine order, where the Immaculate Conception is comparable to super-essential All-Possibility, the more-than-luminous darkness of the Trinity, as well as the hypostatic maternity of the Holy Spirit.

Cosmic charity and the universal Virgin. *Materia prima* is what remains when all *form*, all 'in-formation', is withdrawn. The Form of forms, that is, the *Logos* itself, is the superabundant fullness of the divine possibles facing the poverty of the *materia*. Founded *in Principio* (*"In Principio Deus creavit terram et caelos"*), prime matter is a 'principial' condition. Moreover, St. Thomas states that it is even *co-created* rather than created, which means that it is not the subject of a separate creation, but it accompanies the creation of beings.

This *materia prima* is thus non-informed, universal, pure. Sheer potentiality, absolutely indistinguishable and undifferentiated, it can be rightly said to be unintelligible for man, because there is actually nothing to be known in it. And creatures, since they participate in the potentiality of this *universal substrate*, also harbor a kind of unintelligibility.

As *substrate*, a word deriving from *sub-stare*, literally '*what stands beneath*' (as in sup-port, sup-posit and *sub-stratum*), *materia prima* (this substrate) is not only located below the world but below all worlds, in such a way that, for St. Bonaventure, it is itself angelic matter.

It therefore receives all created forms within itself, but has itself no form and is still *virgin* in relation to all its determinations. As it tirelessly gives itself to all forms it receives, it can be viewed as *cosmic charity*: "the charity which endures all things" (cf. St. Paul), the cosmic receptacle, the very receptivity of the created— "cosmic charity because through it God created the world, that is to say, through it, through this unconceivable alterity which defines it, God projects the pure forms into this other-than-Himself. It is the very substance of cosmic love, since it testifies, through its mysterious nature, that God consents to what is other than Himself."[14]

14 Ibid., 299.

The cosmic matrix is the universal Mother. To God consenting to project the possibles this side of pure Being, that is, this side of *Materia Prima*, corresponds the Divine Word willing to take human form in the womb of the Virgin Mary — which is to say that the uncreated Word, the hypostatic Synthesis of all possible creatures, takes flesh in Mary.

This Work accomplished in Mary is even more prodigious than the Creation of the world, since, by the grace of Christ, it is the whole creation that is restored to its principial splendor.

If Genesis shows the *prima materia* under the symbol of water, this is because "it is apt, like water, to give form to all forms";[15] and, just as in the Beginning the Holy Spirit moved over the primordial waters of universal Existence so that creatures were produced, *Maria* (that is to say 'waters' in Latin) is over-shadowed by the Paraclete so that the Word is conceived in her.

In this way the symbolic equivalences of *Maria, Mater, Materia* and matrix become apparent, since only a virgin creature can be the Mother of the Uncreated, only perfect emptiness can contain total Fullness.[16]

Super-essential All-Possibility is the Immaculate Conception. First, the Infinite Possibility that is God Himself, insofar as He knows Himself as the archetype of everything possible, can be defined as the conception that God has of Himself. God Himself conceives Himself and the fruit of this conception is the infinity of possibilities. Precisely because these possibilities are absolutely infinite, not limited or determined, this divine conception is immaculate.

Next, a creature, preserved from its origins from original sin — this is the creature in all its purity, perfectly conformed to its archetype *in divinis*. And this Immaculate Conception of Mary is also the Immaculate Conception that God has of Mary.

Finally, Mary did not say at Lourdes in 1858 that her conception was immaculate but, rather, "I am the Immaculate Conception" (*"Que soy era Immaculada Counceptiou"*). She is therefore not one immaculate conception among others, but *the* Immaculate Conception herself. Even though Mary is a creature, she becomes a creature apart. If all creatures have in God an uncreated being (their archetype), the uncreated archetype of Mary is the Divine Essence in the way that it conceives all archetypes.

---

15 St. Thomas Aquinas, *Summa Theologiae* I, q. 66, a. 1; cf. *Amour et vérité*, 299.
16 *Amour et vérité*, 299.

She is the human face, the visible symbol of Universal Possibility, of All-Possibility, the infinite Fecundity of the Infinite, in which she mysteriously participates.[17]

The more-than-luminous Darkness of the Trinity is the Immaculate Conception. The Trinitarian unfolding of the Godhead, of the Divine Essence, is the Conception according to which (in the Latin perspective) the Divine Essence is revealed to Itself. This inner matrix of the Divine Essence, this unfathomable depth of the Godhead, the shoreless ocean of absolute Substance, the more-than-luminous Darkness of the super-essential Thearchy, is the immaculate Conception of the eternal unfolding of Trinitarian relationships.

This Conception is perfectly Immaculate since the real distinction of each Hypostasis in no way determines or limits the Godhead, which remains One, Unique, and Infinite in each of Them. The Marian correspondence here brings out the symbolic identification of Mary with this Immaculate Conception that is the very depths of the Trinitarian Essence.[18]

The Hypostatic motherhood of the Holy Spirit is the primordial immaculate Conception. In Catholic tradition, the Word is the Concept, the fruit of the begetting of the Son by the Father, by the mode of knowledge (cf. Saint Augustine). If the Father is the Conceiver and the Son the Concept, the Holy Spirit is the Conception itself: the unifying space by which and in which the Divine Essence as the Father can beget Itself as Son.

The Holy Spirit is Love and Gift (His proper names, according to St. Thomas Aquinas),[19] Love and the hypostatic Gift in which the Father and the Son are united. He is the hypostatic Charity that reveals the Father to the Son and the Son to the Father; He is the passive spiration, the support for the active spiration of the love of the Father and the Son; He is the Divine Essence insofar as It gives Itself and insofar as It is loved. He does not beget but gives birth to the Son for the Father. It is in the Person of the Holy Spirit that is realized the unifying explosion of the Trinity. If the Father is the active source and the monarchic origin of the self-communion of the Divine Essence, the Holy Spirit, the charity-Hypostasis, is the passive condition by which begetting and spiration are co-eternally in act.

---

17 Ibid., 295.
18 Ibid., 296.
19 St. Thomas Aquinas, *Summa Theologiae* I, q. 37, q. 38 a. 1.

This hypostatic motherhood of the Holy Spirit — this hypostatic and immaculate Conception — is the Immaculate Conception. And the Theotokos, the Immaculate Conception, is the image of the Holy Spirit as hypostatic Maternity, which represents one of her functions. She is therefore a manifestation of this Maternity because she is the Mother of God insofar as her divine Prototype exercises this maternal role within the bosom of the divine Trinity. In the historical and truly human Incarnation *ex Maria Virgine*, the Holy Spirit is revealed in Mary who receives from Him, because He possesses the relationship of divine Motherhood from all eternity. "*Filius incarnatus est: Jesus Christus; Spiritus Sanctus quasi-incarnatus est: Immaculata*" (St. Maximilian Kolbe): the incarnation of the Son is Jesus Christ, the manifestation of the Holy Spirit is the Virgin.[20]

20 *Amour et vérité*, 296.